P9-CEN-873

DEDICATION

For my mother, Grace A. Biser, who made it all possible.

For my wife, Beth, and our children,

Jim and Jenni, who make it all meaningful.

Published in 1998 by:
Frank Amato Publications, Inc.
P.O. Box 82112, Portland, Oregon 97282, (503) 653-8108
Softbound UPC: 0-66066-00318-8
Softbound ISBN: 1-57188-120-4
All photographs taken by the author unless otherwise noted.
Cover photo: Underwater redds, William H. Mullins
Book design: Kristi Workman Rossman
Printed in Canada

10 9 8 7 6 5 4 3 2

Kokanee

A Complete Fishing Guide

Dave Biser

Contents

TABLE OF CONTENTS

Section Three: ANGLING METHODS AND TECHNIQUES

continued on page 6...

TABLE OF CONTENTS *continued...*

Section Five: PLACES

Section Six: APPENDIX

ACKNOWLEDGEMENTS

I am indebted to so many for help with this book that I scarcely know where to begin.

Tom Capelli got us started on the right foot in this sport, teaching us the value of light equipment and downriggers. Tom, an excellent guide, showed us many good times early in our kokanee experience.

Then there are the fisheries and wildlife professionals whose help made the book possible. I have file cabinets filled with information from these people. Pat Martinez alone filled one or two drawers, sent me photos, and contributed knowledge I could have obtained nowhere else. Jim Vashro wrote an eloquent summary of the conditions of the kokanee waters in northwestern Montana that has been of great value. Wayne Hadley taught me all I needed to know about Georgetown, sent me lures and equipment unique to that fishery, and kept me laughing with his good Montana jokes. Mike Hatch, an esteemed friend, helped far beyond my ability to repay. Roger Schneidervin and Steve Brayton, other new and valued friends, were always there to answer my many questions. Dana Dewey, Roger Wilson, Mike Japhet, Greg Friday, George Galvan, and others kindly allowed us to help with spawning salmon, educated us about hatcheries, and taught us much about kokanee propagation.

Vaughn Paragamian, Wade Fredenberg, John Hisata, Tim Barry, Rick Jacobson, Bob Hooton, Jake Bennett, Ken Sorenson, Bruce Rieman, Laney Henzel, Dr. Chris Luecki, Tim Peone, Dale Chess, Scott Hebner, Ralph Roseberg, Bill Knox, Mas Yamashita, Steve Anderson, Bob Akroyd, Al Langston, Susan Thompson, Dr. T. G. Northcote, Russ Wickwire, Lance Nelson, Bill Wengert, Marc Wethington, and Paul Cassidy all shared their time freely.

I am in debt to the staff of the library at Utah State University for their help in finding hard to locate papers on the little red salmon. The Farmington, NM public library helped me find many good books and papers through interlibrary loan that would otherwise have been hard to access.

Phil Johnson gave me so much advice and help on technique and tackle that it is hard to imagine the book without the input of this dedicated and successful kokanee angler. Frank Verano taught me much; I sense great kindness in this man. Would I had had the resources to get back there and fish with him. Frank, John Skibsrud, and Joe Hackett helped me greatly on night fishing techniques.

Thanks to Vance Staplin, Chester Bodo, Rob Clifford, and Steve Emrick for their help and interest. Ron Carey supplied good information and photos.

Sep and Marilyn Hendrickson, the tackle makers from Cowtown (Vacaville), California, made us feel welcome in their home and shared tons of articles, photos, knowledge, and equipment. Larry Federici, the Superintendent of Navajo Lake State Park, and his lovely wife Laura, two of the most knowledgeable anglers and hunters in the Southwest, provided unselfishly their time, knowledge, and photos.

Cliff Dare, who owns Kootenay River Outfitters in Troy, spent hours sharing with us his love and knowledge of northwestern Montana, and kept us fascinated with his vast storehouse of rich and interesting stories. Those hours passed much too quickly.

It was Cliff who told us about Ron Raiha, owner of Pend Oreille Sports Shop in Sandpoint, Idaho. Ron, like Cliff, is the kind of person you feel privileged to meet. There are too few people around like Cliff and Ron.

Add to that folks like Roy Bradshaw of Real Images, Doug Phillips of Strawberry Bay Marina, Gary Mirrales of Shasta Tackle, Jeff Borchert of Rainbow Bait in Cortez, Colorado, Cliff Redmon, who guides anglers on Flaming Gorge, all of whom have been extremely helpful. A word of appreciation must go to Idaho biologist and photographer Bill Mullins who has allowed me to keep his valuable kokanee photos far too long.

A sincere thank you to publisher Frank Amato, who has been patient beyond belief as I, for various reasons, have taken an unreasonably long time to finish this book. I also greatly appreciate editor Kim Koch, who has been ready with help and encouragement on so many occasions.

Gary McDowell, a great friend, has been a rich source of encouragement.

Finally my gratitude goes to my wife Beth, my son Jim, my daughter Jenni and my daughter-in-law Debra for their patience and encouragement during the long months of inattention from me. Beth helped with so much of this work, she really should be named co-author, though she rejected the idea.

I know there are other delightful people out there who have helped me and whose names I have omitted. Of them I can only ask that they understand, and know of my gratitude.

Dave Biser
October 1996
Kirtland, New Mexico

INTRODUCTION

Primarily, this is a book about pursuing and catching kokanee salmon. I have tried to include some biology, but hopefully have not strayed too far from the book's main purpose of helping those new to the sport get a good start and helping those with some expertise encounter new ideas to try in their never ending quest to hone their skills. It is humbling to know that, even after all this study and writing, many who will read this book are better kokanee anglers than I.

Recently, to get in the proper spirit to finish up this work, I sneaked off and spent an afternoon in a place I know where thousands of kokanee run up into a bay and on into the creek at its head each fall. They are big and brightly colored, these fish. Snagging is illegal here, so a person seeking peace among these spawners can often find it.

Some of the leaves were still hanging to the trees and shrubs around the lake. The land had not yet lost that wonderful fall yellow/green/red/salmon/orange color and leaf mold scent that it can attain only through the deaths of uncountable numbers of leaves.

Spawning kokanee salmon, the reds of autumn, dominated several bays of the big lake. Sitting in a small boat on one of these bays, I watched as every few seconds a bright red/orange salmon became airborne near me, either jumping high or porpoising along the surface for several yards before disappearing back into the water. The bottom below me was red and in constant motion. I attached a snelled, size 16 treble hook to my line and installed a tiny split shot two feet above it. I molded a gob of Sparkle Pink Power Bait onto the small, gold-plated hook and dropped the rig into the water not far from the boat. The tiny shot pulled the buoyant bait down, but there was resistance. Though it fell, it fell slowly, the way a piece of Styrofoam falls in still air.

The shot had yet to hit bottom when the first koke, a big red female, took it. She went insane, jumping, pulling, making long hard runs that had the drag on the little Garcia singing. I doubted I could hold a fish so large and strong with the tiny hook. She was, it seemed during the next 20 minutes, going to pull free any second, but finally she tired.

On my knees in the boat, I led her quietly to the side, took my needle nose pliers and grabbed the exposed part of the tiny hook. With a flick of my wrist she was free. She lay there for a few seconds, then with a wave of her tail, she disappeared into the moving red mass six feet below.

The scene was repeated several more times before I had played enough kokanee to be satisfied. I released each fish as I had the first. Using the electric trolling motor, I moved slowly to the head of the bay, beached the boat, walked up the stream. Every pool held fifteen or 20 big red fish. Here and there were a few cutthroats, hanging around no doubt in anticipation of munching on kokanee eggs. Or perhaps they came just to see what the heck all the fuss was about.

Finding a low vertical bank that overlooked a still pool, I lay down and belly crawled to the edge. Peering over, I could see several big red bodies near enough to touch. Ever so slowly, like the foot of a stalking heron, my hand eased itself into the water. With a movement that was barely perceptible, it approached the nearest fish, a big, hump-backed male. The backs of my fingers touched his leather side ever so lightly and moved along it. His skin felt good to my hand. Cool, not really smooth, but not rough either.

It was not the skin, but the life within the animal that I really felt. The communication, however limited, with a being of another blood. Touching a rock of the same texture and temperature would not have been the same.

I moved a tad too quickly or touched with a bit too much pressure and spooked him. He shot away, not like a rocket, but like a flying saucer in a sci-fi movie. One of those craft capable of going from 0 to full velocity instantaneously. His fear moved like a wave through all the fish in the pool and all darted around aimlessly for a several seconds. Then there was a collective settling down.

I removed my hand from the cold water, dried it on my sweatshirt, and lay watching the fish until the late afternoon light began to weaken. I sat up, but stayed longer, enjoying the fall air with its faint hint of chill and listening to the sounds of the critters around me. Sleepy birds sang here and there. A western screech owl called. Several deer passed by on the far side of the creek.

During those pleasing, quiet moments, I realized how much I have benefited by getting to know the kokanee salmon. May you and yours, as you come to know the kokanee through studying, catching, handling, and eating him, experience the same enjoyment that has come to me as I have come to know, if only in a small way, this great and ancient race. Good fishing!

Section One

THE FISH

MEET THE KOKANEE

One

NATURAL HISTORY

Over the course of history many varieties of freshwater fish have found ways to utilize the most immense food source on the planet, the oceans. Separating from their relatives, many individuals, at various times in prehistory, have left their freshwater homes and began to spend more and more time in salt water. Gradually, their behavior, food preferences, and physiology have diversified in these huge ecosystems and they been transformed into some of the saltwater fishes we know today. So it was with the ancestors of the fish we now call the Pacific Salmon.

Five living salmon species are descendants of those ancient north Pacific adventurers. They are primarily anadromous, spending their adult lives in the ocean, reproducing in fresh water. They are the coho or silver salmon (*Oncorhynchus kisutch*), the chum or dog (*O. keta*), the pink or humpback (*O. gorbuscha*), the chinook or king (*O. tshawytscha*), and the sockeye or red salmon (*O. nerka*).

These five species vary considerably in size as shown by the all©tackle world records (1994 data): king, 97 lb. 4 oz.; coho, 33 lb. 4 oz.; chum, 32 lb.; sockeye, 15 lb. 3 oz.; and pink, 13 lb. 1 oz. One related, extinct species bore six-inch breeding teeth and grew to eight feet and 240 pounds. The sockeye, while one of the smallest, is also one of the most important to today's commercial fishing industry. If you have eaten canned salmon, you have probably eaten sockeye.

The Salmon-Trout Family

These ancestral salmon and their relatives make up the family Salmonidae. This family is composed of several genera that inhabit cold water in various parts of the world.Like our Pacific salmon, many of these related trout and salmon species show a strong tendency to go to sea.

One related group within this family is the genus *Salvelinus*. It consists of several troutlike species called char, namely the brook trout, the Arctic char, the mackinaw or lake trout, the bull trout, and the Dolly Varden trout. In the Arctic, Dolly Vardens go to sea regularly. Sea©run brook trout are common along the east coast of Canada and New England, and Arctic char spend much of their lives in the ocean.

Another group within this family is the genus *Salmo*. It consists of the Atlantic salmon, which lives in the North Atlantic, spawning in streams in Iceland, Greenland, northern Europe, Great Britain, and North America.Unlike Pacific salmon, most Atlantic salmon do not die after spawning. There is a landlocked form that is a prized game fish in the Northeast. Another member of *Salmo* is the brown trout, often referred to as the German or European brown. Rainbow, golden, cutthroat, Gila, Apache, and other Western species of trout were, until recently, considered members of the genus *Salmo*. Modern technology, such as the study of

DNA through electrophoresis, has shown them to be more properly placed in the genus *Oncorhynchus*, the same genus as the Pacific salmon. The genera *Salvelinus*, *Salmo, Oncorhynchus*, and *Thymallus*, the grayling, are all members of the family Salmonidae.

The Pacific Salmon Today

Migration to the sea has allowed the Pacific salmon to exist in much larger numbers and in larger sizes than would have been likely had they stayed in fresh water. The practice of migrating to fresh water to spawn has allowed young salmon to avoid much of the predation they would face in the ocean. In the last several decades, however, much of this advantage has been negated by the construction of dams on the rivers used by the salmon and the introduction of various freshwater predators such as bass and walleye.

The anadromous lifestyle is fraught with challenges. These include the rigors of long trips upstream, the limited carrying capacity of the cold, clear waters to which the salmon return to reproduce, and the fact that legions of huge fish invading periodically from the ocean could soon consume all the fish in such waters, including the young of their own species produced there in previous years.

The changes salmon undergo at spawning time enable the fish to meet these challenges successfully. The spawner is more able to withstand the long upstream journey because it is a much tougher, stronger fish than it was prior to the spawn.

The problem with the lack of nutrients in the spawning waters is dealt with in an unusual way. Soon after spawning, the salmon start to lose their tenacious grip on life. They then die in the stream. As their bodies decompose, they release nutrients to the local ecosystem that will provide food to support the hordes of young salmon to come.

A species that devoured the bulk of its young from previous years during each spawning run would soon face extinction. The tendency in these fish to not eat during the spawning is therefore advantageous to their survival. For this reason Pacific salmon cease to eat, living off stored fat and parts of their bodies that are not immediately essential to life or to reproduction.

The Kokanee

Sometime after the development of the Pacific salmon, some individuals of the sockeye species began to live out their lives in fresh water. This probably happened, though not necessarily for the first time, since the last ice age. This lacustrine (lake-dwelling) form of the sockeye is called the kokanee salmon. It is of the same species (*Oncorhynchus nerka*) as the sockeye, but has ceased to be anadromous.

In some cases, the young salmon may have been forced to stay in fresh water by geological events that blocked their path to the sea. There is a lot of talk and some writing that hints that *all* kokanee separated from anadromous sockeye stock in this way. Evidence supports the concept, however, that some of the fish simply preferred not to go to the ocean. Many lake systems now have or have had both anadromous sockeye and kokanee living in them.

The kokanee has not lost the sockeye's old ways of reproduction. At the end of two to seven years of life, the kokanee, like the sockeye, undergoes significant

After spawning, kokanee give up their energy and nutrients to the natal stream by dying and being recycled into the environment.

physical changes, spawns, and dies. Though it is typically smaller, a spawning kokanee looks much like a spawning sockeye.

BIOLOGY

From Egg to Adult

Some kokanee spawn in streams, others in lakes. After the spawn, the rotting corpses of the spent adults litter the stream or lake bottom and its banks. A surprising array of species—including whitetail deer—has been seen eating dead or dying kokanee. The rotting corpses that remain uneaten release nutrients into the water and enrich it, enabling the creek and the lakes and rivers downstream to support abundant populations of aquatic insects and other small invertebrates that could not exist without this infusion of nourishment provided by the dying red fish. These small animals will in turn become the food of young salmon and hordes of other creatures.

Kokanee (the name kokanee is derived from a Kootenai—Kootenay in Canada—Indian word meaning "red fish") begin life as small eggs deposited in the fall in gravel nests called redds. Redds are formed by the fish in stream or lake bottom gravel. To be suitable for spawning redds, the gravel must be kept clean by currents or wave action. Silt accumulation on the redd would smother the eggs.

How soon the eggs hatch depends largely on water temperature, colder water causing slower development. Optimum temperatures seem to be in the low 50 degrees F range. Eggs take an average of 60 to 65 days to hatch.

The newly hatched kokanee, called an alevin or sac fry, has a large yolk sack attached to its belly. This feeds the tiny fish for the first few weeks of life as it hides among the gravel of the redd and the nearby stream bottom. Alevins, which average about 15 mm long, occasionally undergo a burst of rapid swimming motion—a sort of spasm—designed to strengthen muscles that will soon be needed for catching prey and escaping predators.

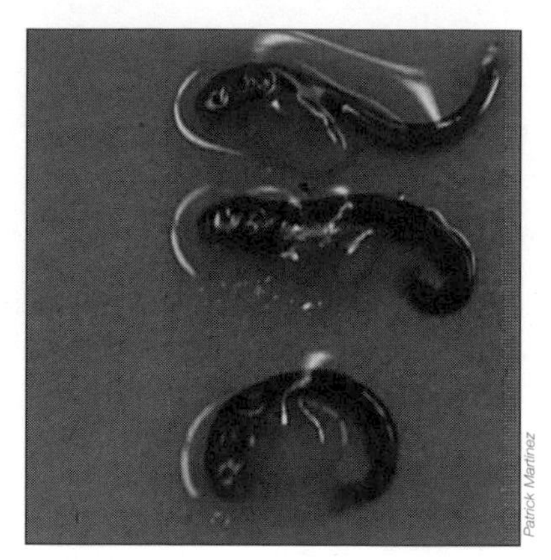
Patrick Martinez

Newly hatched kokanee.

In three to four weeks the young fish will have absorbed their yolk sacks and will average about 20 mm (3/4") long. They will leave the relative safety of the gravel and start feeding on minute plants and animals. At this stage, the fish are called fry.

By mid-spring, the fish are one to one and a half inches long and are called advanced fry. Those in streams move downstream toward the lake. They are often swept into the lake by spring runoff. Those in the edges of lakes come out into open water. In open water, the fish form schools and begin the pelagic, plankton-grazing lifestyle they will live until they spawn two to four years later.

To Adulthood

Most kokanee are considered adults as they enter their third or fourth year, though this varies somewhat according to the availability of nutrition and other factors. In lakes where food is super abundant, kokes may mature and spawn earlier than the norm.

Strawberry Reservoir in north central Utah was treated with rotenone in 1990 to kill off the suckers and Utah chubs that had taken over there. Afterward, one of the species stocked in this big rich lake was the kokanee salmon.

Biologists expected a significant spawn in three years, another in four. But the kokanee, eating like hogs and growing like weeds out in the rich, green, soupy water, did not bother to read the same studies the biologists had. A few small males showed up in the late summer of the first year, all ready to spawn.

The second year showed a good healthy spawn, the participants in which should not have spawned for at least another year. Strawberry has since become the playground of some huge kokanee, producing several over six pounds.

The early maturing of the Strawberry kokanee is not uncommon where food is very abundant. Age at maturity seems to vary inversely with availability of nourishment and rate of growth, but is also affected by genetics.

Lake and River Spawning

Kokanee and young sockeye often live in the same lakes, though there is no evidence that they have any interaction with one another, aside from competing for the same food. Recent research by Canadian biologists seems to indicate that there are subtle genetic differences, not only between sockeye and kokanee, but between individual strains of kokanee that spawn in lakes and those that spawn in streams. There are even genetic differences between sockeye that spawn in rivers above lakes and live a year or two in the lakes and those that spawn downstream from a lake. And these downstream spawners are further divided into those that stay for a time in the river and those that go very soon to the ocean.

Sockeye that spawn in the upper reaches of a drainage typically spawn earlier than those that spawn in a lake or downstream of a lake. We see similar differences in populations of kokanee that have been transplanted by man. Kokanee that spawn in Sheep Creek, a tributary of Flaming Gorge Reservoir, for example, spawn in late August through early October. Another variety spawns in certain exposures of broken shale in the lake in late fall and winter.

The Transformation to Spawner

Kokanee typically travel only a few miles upstream to spawn. Anadromous sockeye often travel many hundreds of miles from the ocean to spawning grounds. Consider, for example, the sockeye that once spawned in Redfish and Stanley lakes in Idaho, and Wallowa Lake in eastern Oregon. Not only was the distance great, the change in elevation was considerable.

Hydroelectric dams have virtually put a stop to most salmon journeys up our major Northwestern rivers. In August of 1992 the arrival of Lonesome Larry, the only sockeye salmon to make it to Redfish Lake in Idaho that year, touched the hearts of thousands. Larry had fought his way up through hundreds of miles of strong current and probably seven or eight major dams, but there was no one with whom he could mate.

Kokanee undergo a prespawn transformation that serves them well as they ascend small streams to spawn, or as they compete with other kokanee for spawning sites. The scales, part of which seem to be metabolized for energy, imbed deeply into the skin and are covered with a layer of mucous as tough as vinyl. Internal organs not immediately essential to life are absorbed into the body and used to provide the incredible amounts of energy or to build the extra muscle needed. Males develop hooked jaws and humped backs; color changes from shiny silver to bright or mottled red or orange on the body and dark green on the head.

Immature kokanee, and even adults that will spawn soon but have not yet begun their metamorphosis, are delicate fish. They lose scales readily upon handling. Survival rates of kokanee caught and released are extremely low.

The salmon that is ready to spawn is a super fish. He or she can be battered against rocks by big rivers without serious harm, can travel hundreds of miles against strong currents without eating. Spawners can be caught and handled, photographed, even stripped of eggs or milt, and will be chipper as can be upon being returned to the water. Handled fish do seem to succumb more quickly to the fungus infections that attack all dying kokanee, however.

After spawning, or before, if they take too long in their journey, the deterioration of the spawners accelerates. White spots of fungus appear, and the fish become visibly less energetic than they were hours before, when they seemed ready to take on anything. Soon they die and give up their nutrients to the stream, or to whatever eats them.

Feeding Habits and Habitat Preferences

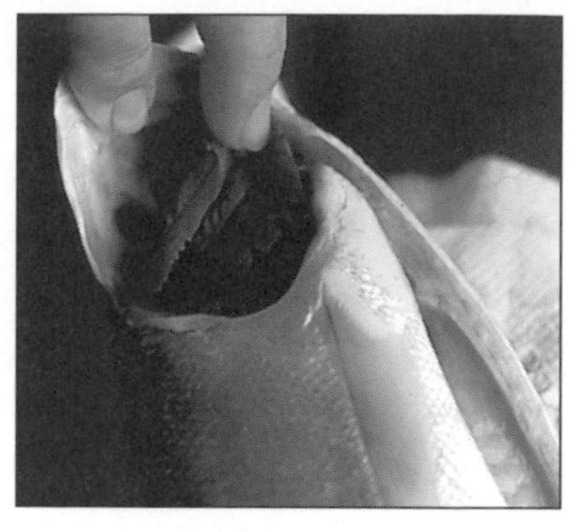

Gill rakers, the white projections inside the gills, serve to filter plankton from the water.

Sockeye and kokanee are pelagic (open water) grazers. They cruise about in open water instead of frequenting structure and cover as do many other fish. As they cruise, they consume zooplankton that they filter from the water with their gill rakers.

The gills of kokanee have very efficient rakers, small projections resembling the teeth of a comb. Most fish have these, but in kokanee, they are larger and more numerous than in say, rainbow trout. The rakers filter the larger zooplankton out of the water as it passes over their gills.

Kokanee do not just blindly filter water, but go after individual prey as does a trout or bass. It is just that their prey are often so small that the koke has to allow them to pass through the mouth and catch it with the gill rakers.

Kokanee hit lures with reckless abandon. To troll a small, shiny, fluttering spoon, or a bright spinner by a kokanee when it is in the mood is to nearly have the rod jerked from your hand.

Why do you think a fish that eats plankton would attack a minnow, or a lure that imitates one? I have posed this question to many anglers, guides, and biologists without getting an answer backed by conclusive evidence. Several biologists have assured me that kokanee do eat fish. I know of no one, however, who has found a small fish in the stomach of a kokanee. I have copies of the results of surveys of the stomach contents of hundreds of kokanee that did not turn up a single small fish.

Kokanee typically go into one of the best bites of the year in late spring as the plankton blooms become more prevalent. The blooms of phytoplankton, combined with favorable temperature and light conditions, jump start the growth and reproduction of *Daphnia*, the kokanee's favorite brand of zooplankton. The increased abundance of *Daphnia* in turn fires up the appetite of the kokanee.

PLANKTON

One often hears that kokanee eat plankton. But what exactly is plankton? How big are these critters? What do they look like? How do they behave?

Plankton consists of clouds of tiny plants and animals that live suspended in fresh or saltwater. They range in size from microscopic to an inch or more in length. Some of these critters can swim on their own power while others just drift along, but all bona fide members of the plankton community depend on currents of wind and water for their general direction and speed of travel. The plankton in a lake may include hundreds of species of plants and animals.

The portion of a plankton population that is made up of plant life is called phytoplankton. These tiny plants, many of which are one-celled and cannot be seen in any detail without a microscope, represent the foundation of the food web of any body of water. The importance of these plants cannot be overstressed. The lives of virtually all the creatures in the lake depend on them.

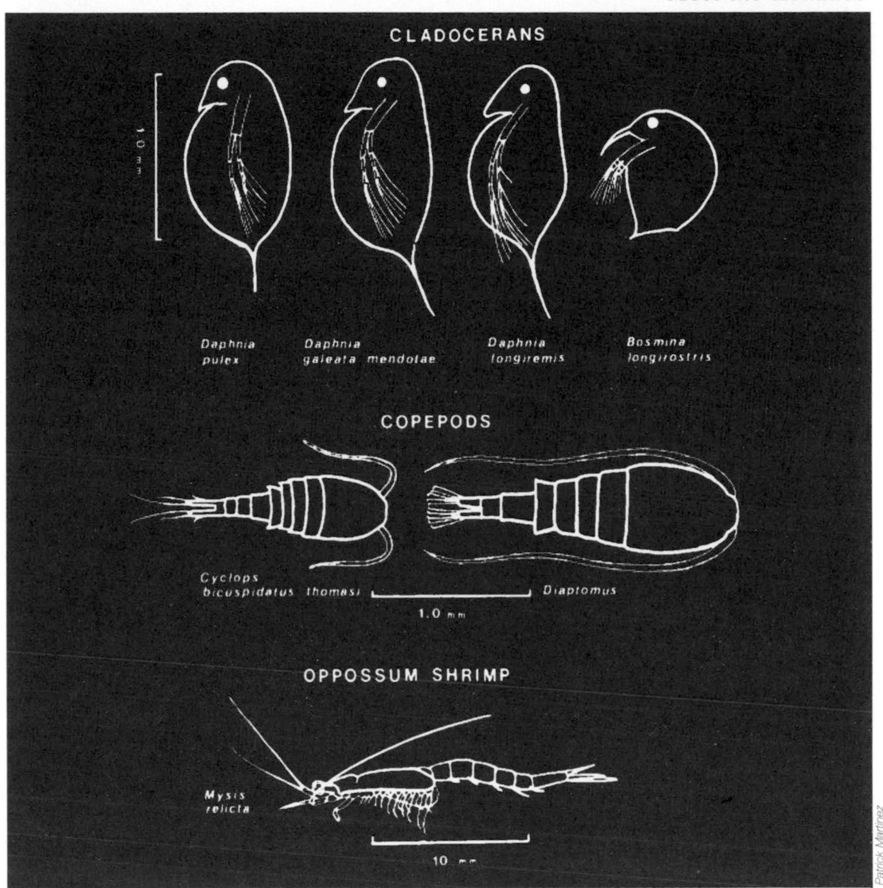

Two of the most important members of the plankton community to the kokanee angler are Daphnia *and* Cyclops. Mysis relicta, *the opossum shrimp, is not a bona fide member of the community; it just stops by once in a while for lunch.*

Phytoplankton in the oceans is responsible, along with our dwindling forests, for most of the free oxygen in our atmosphere, on which we and most other life forms depend. Through photosynthesis, phytoplankton captures the energy of photons of light from the sun and transforms it into the stored energy of chemical bonds. This is the energy that fuels the tiny plants themselves and everything above them in the food web of that lake.

Munching constantly on the phytoplankton (and on each other) are zooplankters, the small animals that live in this diminutive floating jungle. They include representatives of several groups of animals, such as insects and their larvae, crustaceans, flat worms, and nematodes. There are rotifers, strange little animals that move about by rotating cilia on their bodies. Odd little critters such as hydra, related to sea anemones, consume other small animals.

There are also creatures that are classified as members of kingdoms other than the plant and animal kingdoms. They are mostly one-celled little protozoa and bacteria. Some act like animals in that they are free swimming, but also carry on photosynthesis as do green plants.

Of major interest directly to the kokanee and therefore to us as kokanee anglers, are several creatures that are members of the class we call Crustacea. This class of animals also includes shrimp, crabs, lobsters, crayfish, and sow bugs. Two of the most prominent orders within this class are the Cladocera (water fleas), tiny upright swimming critters that max out at 3mm and roughly resemble little round seeds, and free-living Copepoda, animals of about the same size, many of which resemble miniature shrimp or horseshoe crabs.

Daphnia

Several species of the genus *Daphnia* (order Cladocera) make up a large part of the kokanee salmon's diet. *Daphnia* tend to swim slowly, while some of the Copepoda are quite fast. Thus the *Daphnia*, being easier to catch, and perhaps tasting better—who knows?—figures more heavily in the diet of the kokanee and several other creatures.

Daphnia typically suspend in water in an upright position, with the head to the top. They are nearly round, with legs and antennae sticking out here and there. They are covered across the back and sides by a shell that they secrete. The shell is open in front, somewhat like a raincoat or robe that is not buttoned. The critters move in jerky little "hops" by rowing with their antennae. They feed by waving their legs and creating a current of water through their shells, then filtering from that water small pieces of organic detritus, algae, bacteria, and protozoa. So efficient are they at this art that some species can separate tiny colloidal organic particles from the water. Such particles would pass through all but the finest man-made filters.

Any given group of *Daphnia* will usually be made up primarily of one species. If more than one is present, one species will typically outnumber all others by at least 20 to 1. Three common species eaten by kokanee are *Daphnia rosea, D. magna*, and *D. pulex*. *D. pulex* seems to be the koke's favorite in many waters.

These creatures commonly live from one to three months, but live longer in times of low temperature. They tend to be very scarce in lakes in the winter, depending on food supply. In really cold waters, all the adults will die, with only eggs living over the winter to hatch in spring.

Daphnia reproduce largely by parthenogenesis, the process wherein females give birth to offspring from unfertilized eggs. For most of the year, the *Daphnia* population in a given water is composed primarily of parthenogenetic females. Males appear in abundance in late spring, following an explosion in the population of parthenogetic females.

The appearance of the males is followed by the appearance of sexual females. Then the fun begins as the production of fertilized eggs gets underway. This lasts only for a brief period in spring and early summer, and, in some waters, again in late summer or early fall.

Over the year any given *Daphnia* population will be very low to nonexistent in winter, exploding in late spring to a high peak (occasionally to a density of 200 to 500—but more commonly 20 to 30—*Daphnia* per liter of water), thinning out in summer with a possible second peak in early fall, and then the decline to winter scarcity. Most of that time the population will consist primarily of females.

Most species of *Daphnia* are eurythermal, able to withstand wide variations in

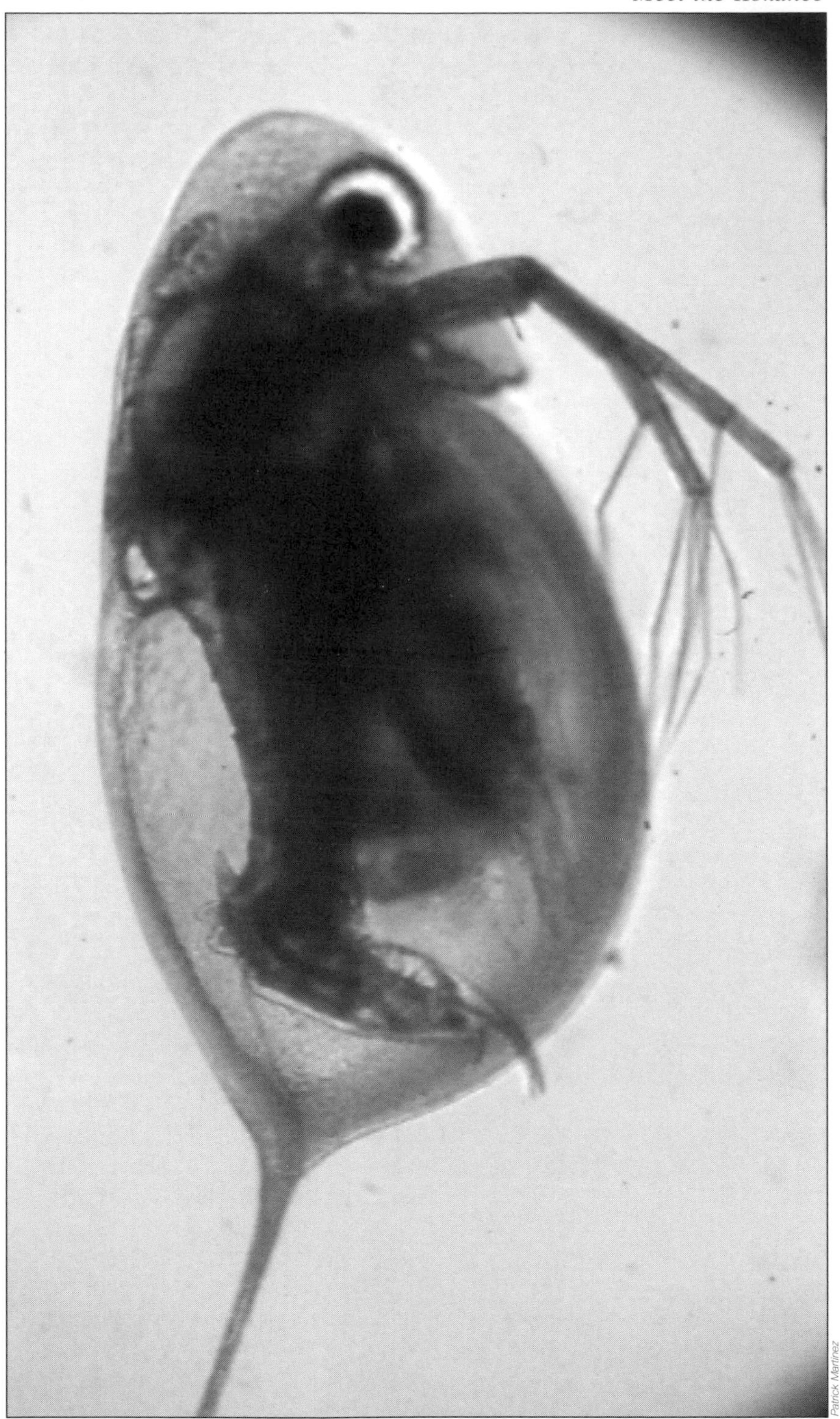

Patrick Martinez

A nice, fat, tasty Daphnia. *Food fit for king kokanee.*

temperature. Many populations undergo vertical migrations every 24 hours, moving closer to the surface at night and sinking deeper at daylight. Some species in certain conditions may move downward at dark and upward come daylight. Kokanee and other plankton eaters often follow these migrations, where temperature permits.

It may seem obvious that these migrations, which may be as far as 30 or 40 feet, are based on a reaction of the *Daphnia* to light. But these animals have been shown to continue their migrations where they were cut off entirely from natural light. Cladocera in general and *Daphnia* in particular are of extreme importance in the food chain of a lake. Studies of the food contents of the stomachs of young fish of various species show up to 95 percent by volume Cladocera, with very few showing less than 10 percent.

Kokanee and other predators of *Daphnia* typically prey on larger individuals. Using this fact, fisheries biologists can often get a handle on the ability of the plankton community in a lake to support more plankton grazers. They take samples of the lake's plankton and grade the *Daphnia* according to size. If a sampling shows a shortage of individuals over 1 mm in length, that is a possible sign that predation on them is becoming stressful. An abundance of big *Daphnia* from 1 to 3 mm would show an ability to support more consumers.

This knowledge may shed light on one possible cause for slow growth of fish in a lake or predict a crash in a population of fish. It is also used to tailor stocking programs to the ability of the lake to support more fish.

Terry Wygart

Mysis relicta*, the opossum shrimp, has had a significant influence on many kokanee populations.*

Mysis relicta

Another creature that, though not a bona fide member, has much to do with some plankton communities is *Mysis relicta*, the opossum shrimp or *Mysis* shrimp, as it is often called. Every kokanee angler should know this guy; every kokanee biologist knows him well already. This critter was originally an inhabitant of certain clear, oligotrophic lakes of the northern United States and Canada. It is also found in northern Eurasia.

Mysis relicta grows to a size of about 1.25 inches (30mm) and it is a voracious predator of *Daphnia* and other zooplankters. Like the kokanee, it seems especially fond of the larger *Daphnia*.

The name opossum shrimp comes from the fact that the creature has a pouch, or marsupium. Eggs and then the young are reared in the pouch until they reach a length of about 3 to 4 mm.

Having evolved in glacial waters, *Mysis relicta* is strictly a cold-water animal. It is typically unable to tolerate water temperatures higher than about 14 degrees C , when lakes are normally stratified.

The presence of *Mysis* shrimp usually tends to negatively impact kokanee for two reasons. One is that the *Mysis* eats plankton, and like the kokanee prefers nice fat *Daphnia. Daphnia* populations often change in content as *Mysis* become established in a lake, with some species practically disappearing. In Dillon Reservoir in Colorado and in huge Flathead Lake in Montana, the proliferation of opossum shrimp had a marked effect on *Daphnia* populations and in turn on kokanee salmon survival.

Even worse, the shrimp migrates vertically each day to avoid predation by the kokanee. At night, when kokanee do not feed unless aided by artificial light, opossum shrimp come as near the surface as temperature will allow and munch freely on *Daphnia* and other plankton. In the daytime, the *Mysis* goes very deep, usually too deep for the kokanee to find and eat it.

By being an ideal forage species for young lake trout, *Mysis* have an even more drastic effect on kokanee in many lakes. While staying deep in the daylight hours enables the shrimp to avoid predation by kokanee salmon, it does not save him from the mackinaw. Lake trout typically hang out at much greater depths than do kokanee, where they eat *Mysis* and grow very quickly to a size at which they can begin to enjoy one of their other favorite foods—kokanee salmon.

Kokanee grow to this size—note 20-inch mark on ruler—by eating well. Big kokes like this Flaming Gorge specimen can indicate small populations or an abundant food supply.

SIZE AT MATURITY

The size of a mature adult kokanee varies greatly based somewhat on growing season, but much more on the availability of food. Food availability is normally based on the fertility of the water and on the number of mouths around to eat the food.

Kokanee can become short of food as a result of competition from other pelagic grazers. The *Mysis* shrimp is a common culprit, but not the only one.

In East Twin Lake, Connecticut, the alewife was introduced illegally. The alewife, a small ocean fish, is very good at grazing plankton and has a tremendous tendency to overpopulate. East Twin was one of the most fertile kokanee lakes in the East before the alewife came along. The alewife appears to have out-competed the kokanee for plankton. The kokanee are gone from East Twin.

Kokanee can also get into a food shortage as a result of overpopulation—"victims of their own too much," as Aldo Leopold said of the overabundant deer of the Kaibab Plateau in northern Arizona. There are many lakes in which kokanee have stunted due to overpopulation.

Sometimes lakes are so poor in nutrients that kokanee have no chance at all of growing large. In western British Columbia and elsewhere many lakes are extremely oligotrophic, or nutrient-poor. Kokanee in some of these bodies of water may mature at a length of six inches.

Temperature also has much to do with rate of growth in fish. In Moon Lake, Utah, low water temperature may be a significant factor in the small size of the kokanee. The lake has unusually cold water for the area.

Occasionally a kokanee is caught whose size is difficult to explain. In Lake Hattie, near Laramie, Wyoming in the fall of 1995, an angler took a kokanee that apparently weighed over eight pounds. Not thinking of records, the angler butchered the fish. Weighed later without head and viscera, the big red fish broke the state record by more than a pound.

Some feel that these were sterile kokanee that lived to be very old, and that that is the reason for their huge size. Sterilized kokanee in McPhee Reservoir, Colorado, and in other waters, however, have gotten only slightly larger than their spawning cohorts, though they have lived several years longer.

RANGE

Kokanee salmon originally occurred in lakes from Alaska down through British Columbia, Washington, Oregon, Idaho and probably Northern California as far south as the Klamath or maybe even the Sacramento River system. They also occur naturally in river systems such as the Anadyr in northeastern Asia and south into Japan.

Because they are wonderful game and food fish, all five species of the Pacific salmon have been and continue to be transplanted widely. Almost certainly the most famous Pacific salmon transplant project was the introduction in the 1960s of various species into the Great Lakes.

The introduction of Pacific salmon into the Great Lakes had been tried unsuccessfully at least twice before, in the late 1800s and again in the 1930s. Several factors, however, led up to the astonishing success of the 1960s effort.

Fisheries scientists on the Great Lakes were led to look for other game fish when the lake trout fishery failed. It had long been a dependable source of sport and income for many people, then the sea lamprey invaded the lakes and the mackinaw fell victim to this parasite, as well as to gross over-fishing.

Too, there was a huge abundance of prey species, particularly rainbow smelt and alewives. Both had become outrageously overpopulated during the scarcity of mackinaw. The alewife, a native of the Atlantic Ocean, entered the lakes through a shipping canal. It was estimated at one time that the alewife made up 90 percent of the total fish biomass in the lakes.

Michigan introduced coho salmon into tributaries of Lakes Michigan, Superior and Huron as five-inch smolts in May of 1966. When the coho and chinook salmon were introduced into these alewife- and herring-filled waters, they found themselves in a paradise where there was more food than a salmon had ever dreamed possible. Some of these salmon, particularly in the relatively warm water of Lake Michigan, were 17 inches long by fall.

By the following fall there were salmon present that weighed over 11 pounds. Within a few years the Great Lakes salmon fishery was famous for its trophy cohos and chinooks. Though food is not so abundant as it was, the fishery still rivals salmon fisheries in the Pacific Northwest.

But kokanee did not fare so well. Today, if there are kokanee in the Great Lakes, the schools are few and scattered.

Kokanee have been introduced into several other places in North America. Alaska, British Columbia, California, Colorado, Connecticut, Idaho, Montana, Nevada (only in Tahoe), New Mexico, New York, Oregon, Utah, Washington, Wyoming, and the Yukon have viable populations today. Many of these, even in the states where kokanee occur naturally, are introduced populations, sustained in many cases by the planting of hatchery stock.

Section Two

EQUIPMENT, BAIT, AND TACKLE

BOATS AND ACCESSORIES

TWO

ONE WAY TO START

My first trip for kokanee was with a friend who had an old aluminum V-bottom boat about 14 feet long. It had a 6-horse Montgomery Ward motor on it and a cheap trolling motor that had just enough thrust to cause the boat to stand still in a weak breeze.

He had no fish finder, no downriggers, but my friend knew the lake and was well aware of where the fish were hanging out. He also knew the approximate depth at which he needed to troll at any given time of year. He updated this information before each fishing trip by talking to a friend at a nearby tackle shop. His units of measure for depth were "colors", which represented the 10-yard colored sections on the lead-core line we were using.

We motored out into Navajo Lake, bouncing over waves that seemed to me entirely too high for the boat we were in. I had been a river fisherman most of my life and was accustomed to standing or sitting on something more solid than this pitching, yawing, rocking, bucking little aluminum horse trough. The shore looked awfully far away.

We started trolling slowly, the old motor belching smoke and decibels into the atmosphere (the electric troller was in the shop that day). As instructed, I threaded some grains of canned yellow corn onto a hook that was attached to the end of a line on which several beads and a small spinner blade were strung. The hook had a gob of pink plastic on the shank below the eye. I had no idea what that was for. It looked like someone's discarded ABC (already been chewed) Bazooka bubble gum. I silently wondered if kokanee liked to blow bubbles.

One of the beads on the monofilament shaft was a tiny ring studded with reflectors made to resemble fake diamonds. I had never before seen a lure built on a piece of monofilament. "What is this thing?"

"Wedding ring spinner. Kokes love it."

About two feet ahead of the lure was a four-inch section of surgical tubing with a swivel at each end. The leading end of that was attached to a gang spinner that had four big spinner blades on it and was about three feet long. I dropped the huge bulk of terminal tackle into the water on the starboard side and shifted the lever on the big Penn reel to free the spool. The heavy, colorful lead-core line started peeling slowly off the reel, gaining speed as more line entered the water and increased the drag. I watched, counting colored 10-yard sections, as the thick line trailed farther and farther behind us. The line farther out was disappearing into the green/clear water.

"Let it out four colors," Chuck counseled.

"How do you know?"

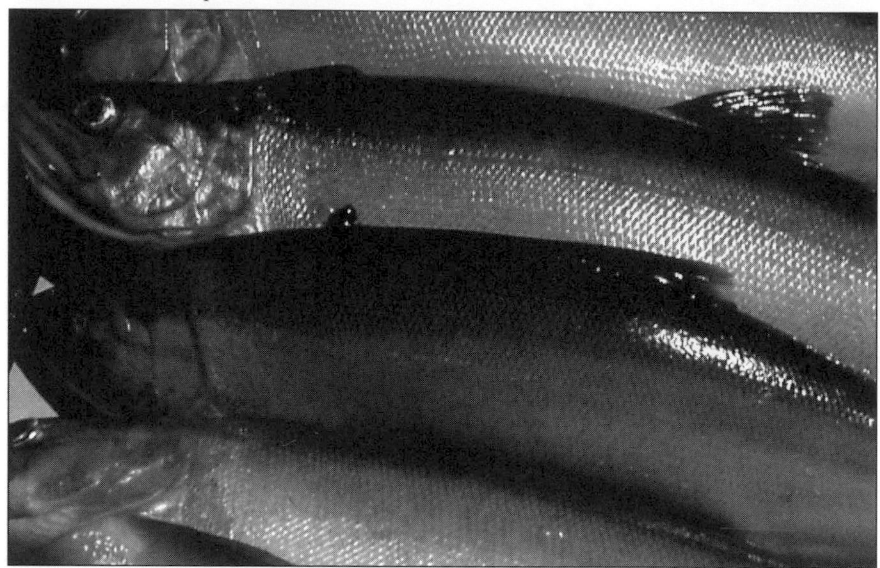

A nice catch of kokanee is a prize sought by thousands of anglers every summer day on hundreds of lakes.

"Trust me." I did as instructed, and engaged the reel.

The drag of all that tackle caused the rod to bow considerably, and the tip kept bobbing. The boat lost about half a knot as the resistance of the water on all that hardware took effect. I was beginning to wonder how one would know if a anything smaller than a Volkswagen hit the lure, when the rod bent a little sharper. The tip started jerking more quickly, more irregularly, more violently.

"You got a fish on, partner!" Chuck yelled. "Don't try to set the hook. Just reel him in slowly and gently. Try to keep the rod perpendicular to the line."

I did as instructed, surprised at how much of the fish's struggle I was able to feel through all that gear. Finally I could see my first kokanee, shining in the water, looking for all the world like pure silver. Chuck had the net ready. I pulled a little harder; so did the koke. Then the silver fish was gone. Straight quiet rod, no life in the line, it was as if the whole episode had never occurred.

"Ya gotta be real gentle with 'em. Their mouths are really soft. Just take your time. Don't try to gain line when they are pulling hard. You may even have to give them line sometimes when they get real feisty. Play them like a big fish that is about to break your line."

It took me about an hour to bring the next one close to the boat. "Not that slow," said Chuck, finishing his third can of pop since the koke had taken the lure. He netted the fish. "Think I'm too old to ketch any more?" he needled.

I began to get the hang of it after a few more fish, some of which made it to the net. By day's end, we had a good bunch of them in the cooler, buried in crushed ice. Chuck explained that it ruins them to put them in a live well or a basket and tow them around in the warm surface water. "They stay good to eat on the ice. They spoil quickly outside the cooler." I had noticed that he had been burying the dead ones in the ice as he put each newly caught koke in the cooler. I also noticed he wore a small woolen glove with which to handle the slippery fish.

Later, after having pursued kokes alone and with Chuck and other friends for a few months—I was beginning to become addicted—I met Tom Capelli, a fishing guide on Heron Lake. Heron is a clear, cold, 6000-acre body of water in northern New Mexico. Heron holds the distinction of being, to my knowledge, the southernmost lake in the West that holds mackinaw. I had been assigned a magazine article on fishing for mackinaw in Heron, and Tom had been recommended to me as the best and most sociable guide on that lake.

I still do not know exactly why Tom granted me an interview, or why he later invited me to go fishing for kokanee. He had had some bad experiences with writers before that and had decided not to or work with writers anymore. I am really glad for the lapse of memory or for the pity he took on me that caused him to change his mind. He is one of the people to whom I was referring when I said that getting to know them would have been adequate compensation for doing the book.

Tom played professional football for the Forty-Niners, then became an engineer at Los Alamos Laboratories before retiring and becoming what he really wanted to be, a fishing guide. And he is a very good one. He has the right personality for the job, is outgoing, has a good sense of humor, and can make any trip a good experience. He also knows how to catch fish; his clients typically come back again and again.

He loves to goad me when we are out on Heron on a beautiful day, catching fish, soaking up sun rays, and breathing fresh, clean air, by saying something like, "Man, I live up here. I can do this every day." The emphasis of course is on the fact that I have a day job, which, on occasion, after having read my latest article, he advises me not to quit.

It was Tom who showed my wife Beth, my daughter Jenni, and me how to catch kokanee using downriggers and small dodgers instead of lead line and heavy lake trolls. We fished with light spinning and casting gear and 8-pound monofilament line. We could really feel the fight of these fine fish when we caught them.

Tom occasionally grilled some kokes in foil on his boat and we ate them hot off the grill on paper plates with Ranch Style Beans. That was some of the best fish we had ever tasted. Eaten fresh out of the cold water and in good company and a pleasant environment, it was all the better.

Tom's boat at that time was an older pontoon boat of 24 feet. The plywood floor had been removed by a previous owner and replaced with heavy redwood flooring. There were cracks between the floor boards and when waves came up onto the boat, the water disappeared quickly through the cracks. This attribute reminded me of Thor Heyerdahl's descriptions of the Kon Tiki, the raft Heyerdahl and his associates used to cross much of the Pacific Ocean back in 1947. I specifically remembered Heyerdahl's description of large waves coming aboard during a storm and disappearing harmlessly between the logs of the raft.

Tom had the boat well rigged with a good Bottom Line fish finder and four pedestals onto which Cannon Easi-Troll II downriggers fit. He had a huge rod rack up under the canopy that held rods of all descriptions. He now has a new, 24-foot Smokercraft pontoon boat, similarly equipped.

My wife, daughter, and I fished many times with Tom. It was he who really got us started right in kokanee angling. We delighted in these hard-muscled, fiercely fighting, swift, silvery fish with their soft mouths, hard muscles, and delicious flesh. The more we caught them, the more we wanted to catch.

We bought and sold several boats in the years that followed. All were deep-V styles, and we were never really satisfied with any, though we had fun with all. Then, when I decided to write the book, we began traveling and fishing lakes all over the West. Thus we rented and used boats of every conceivable description from canoes to big pontoons.

My opinion, after all this experience, is that the most desirable large boat for this sport on most medium to large waters is the pontoon boat, at least for our purposes. One can walk around on a pontoon boat. If well designed, it will handle the rough waters of Western lakes fairly well, though not like the big center consoles. It is ideal for camping, or for having fun with a bunch of people on board. On night fishing trips the extra space on a pontoon allows anyone who gets tired to go take a nap and come back and fish later.

Pontoons cost no more than other big boats, less than many. And one can get by well with a smaller motor than is needed with another boat of comparable size. Motors are usually where the real serious costs of boating are encountered.

A fellow angler named Steve Emrick bought an excellent pontoon boat for this kind of angling. It is a Playcraft, set up specifically for fishing. A 20-footer, it has tall, slender pontoons; some feel they handle rough water better than the round pontoons. With a 75-horse Mariner behind it, it will zip right along at over 20 miles per hour.

A highly skilled and experienced angler who has fished all kinds of water around the country, Steve had wanted a large deep-V when he bought the Playcraft, but purchased the pontoon boat because his family wanted one. Now he tells me he would not trade for a deep-V. He has fished lakes from Navajo in New Mexico to Coeur d'Alene in Idaho with the boat and has found it easy to transport and completely capable of handling any situation on the water. Beyond that there is the added comfort of all that extra space.

The Playcraft has plenty of seating and locked storage. A friend installed four pedestals onto which Steve attached bases for his Cannon downriggers. A Humminbird Wide Vision finder and fore and aft trolling motors complete the rig.

Since I wrote the first draft of this chapter, Steve and his family have purchased Glendo Minnow Bucket (307/735-4626), a fine bait and tackle store in Glendo, Wyoming. If you want to get into some really great walleye, channel cat, and trout fishing, you should check out Glendo Lake. Steve's daughter caught a 9-pound rainbow shortly after the family moved into the town. Steve has guides working out of his shop and will see that you have a good trip.

The big V-bottomed rough water boats typically used by walleye fishermen make fine kokanee boats. These are often advertised and sold as "walleye boats." They handle rough water well and are usually equipped with the hardware needed to successfully take kokanee. They come well recommended for the rough and potentially dangerous waters on our big Western lakes.

Probably the most popular boat with the majority of kokanee anglers, is a good, stable, mid-size, tiller-driven V-bottom. Chester Bodo, a very successful New Mexico angler, has a Lund 14-foot aluminum V-bottom boat equipped with two

A good aluminum V-bottom, if well equipped and not overloaded, makes an adequate kokanee fishing vessel.

Walker downriggers on swivel bases and a Humminbird Wide Vision finder. It has a 30-horse Mercury in back.

On the other end of the spectrum is a broad-beamed, flat bottomed canoe. The one I have in mind is an Old Town Discovery 160K. This stable canoe is ideal for smaller waters. There are many fine small lakes that hold good populations of kokanee.

Other possibilities for very small craft are lakes without good access roads or concrete boat ramps. Lakes like 1300-acre Hell Hole in California where there are few large boats or 6000-acre Heron in New Mexico with its "No Wake" rule are good examples. One has to watch the weather and avoid getting caught in a storm.

On Heron, I have often seen the Genesis III Folding "Porta-Botes" in use by kokanee anglers. Though Heron is fairly big at 6000 acres and can get rough, some of the better kokanee fishing is only a short run from shore. Equipped with an electric trolling motor or small gasoline motor, a good portable fish finder, and one or two manual downriggers, this is a great kokanee boat for small waters.

On Strawberry Reservoir in northern Utah, all the marinas are owned by one man. His name is Doug Phillips. He and his son make fishing boats from wood. They use these for inexpensive rentals at their marinas. They have other small skiffs and several pontoons, but most who have used the wood boats prefer them to the commercially made models.

These are among the most satisfactory small fishing boats I have used anywhere. They are 16 feet long and broad of beam. They are quite heavy and very stable. There really is something about wood: the feel of secure stability due to the mass of the boat, the quiet "thump" when you bump something on a gunwale or the bottom. Every angler should fish from one of these boats at least once in his or her life. One begins to think of Santiago, Hemingway's character in *Old Man and the Sea.*

These boats are stable platforms, comfortable for standing or sitting. They do very well in rough water. If you use one, however, be sure of your life preservers; these boats, if swamped, will not hold you up.

Another type of boat we have often encountered in our travels on kokanee lakes is the old fiberglass tri-hull. These boats seem to show up wherever there are kokanee, though they are doubtless used extensively for other fishing also. They appear to work very well on most lakes, are very stable fishing platforms, and can often be bought with a decent motor for a very reasonable price.

Many bass anglers have become interested in kokanee in the last few years. The bass boats they have used for stalking largemouths work admirably as kokanee boats. They typically have large gasoline motors, trolling motors, and decent electronics. Some already have downriggers.

If you do not know boats and boating safety, take a Coast Guard approved course. After your training, go out with experienced folks whom you trust and get a feel for the sport before you venture out alone or with others of limited experience. If you have to, hire a guide and allow him or her to teach you the ropes. People die every year on our big Western lakes; much of that death is due to inexperience.

DOWNRIGGERS

One of the biggest advantages of downriggers is that you can fish with a light outfit with a minimum of hardware on the line. You feel the fight of these hard-fighting fish much more than with a heavy rig equipped with lead line and a lake troll.

Another advantage is that you can reach them regardless of the depth. You can troll with a downrigger at 100 feet or more. You cannot do this with lead line.

Jeff Pederson

A downrigger, a fish finder, and a high-quality light rod and reel form the heart of a kokanee fishing outfit.

My downriggers are Cannon Easi-Troll 2s. These are manual downriggers, costing about $130 each, that have a good clutch and a quality depth indicator. They are made by Computrol, the same Idaho company that makes Bottom Line fish finders. Their quality is excellent, and models are available from a tiny manual costing about $60 to units with electric motors that cost hundreds. Other companies that make quality downriggers include Walker, Big Jon, Scotty, and Penn.

Consider electric downriggers. Unlike the manuals, they leave your hands free to handle your fishing rig. Some of the electrics—this is true of the new Cannons—have positive ion control built in. This feature generates a field of positive ions in the water around the downrigger ball. Such fields have been found to be attractive to fish.

Positive Ion Control

Just as fish are attracted by positive ions, they are repelled by negative charges. Often, the current flow from a boat's battery to the water via the downrigger cable generates negative charges on the downrigger ball and in the surrounding water.

Phil Johnson, the expert California angler whose tips and ideas appear throughout this book, takes steps to insulate his downrigger from leakage from his batteries. Such leakage is the cause of the negative charge accumulation around the downrigger ball. He uses a voltmeter to monitor current flow from his boat to the downrigger. Phil has found that a current flow of more than 0.6 volts from battery to downrigger cable will repel fish. Many aluminum boats release over a volt to the water. Phil recommends keeping the insulation on all wiring in top shape to eliminate leakage.

Several companies are making "black boxes" designed to hook into the downrigger and generate a positive field around the downrigger ball. This is called positive ion control. As mentioned in the section on downriggers, Cannon has incorporated this technology into its better electric downriggers.

Rod Holders

Each downrigger you purchase should have its own rod holder. It is also a good idea to have a few quality rod holders placed in strategic locations around the boat. Take a look at some of the boats set up by professional guides to get some ideas for setting up your own.

ELECTRONICS

For a decent, inexpensive fish finder, and especially if you are using a small craft, consider the Fishin' Buddy II, by Bottom Line. I have one that has served me well for over a year, though it is not the equivalent of a large unit. It has been kicked around, bounced across the bed of a pickup, dropped in the water, and subjected to all types of abuse. All without a malfunction. It is handy because transducer and finder are housed in one casing. It is simple and easy to use, and looks for fish to one side as well as below. I have used it on several types of boats, including pontoon boats.

If you have a large boat of your own, buy the best electronics you can afford. Commercial units start at about $1000 and will pay for themselves in terms of fish found and caught. These big powerful units allow you to scan a wide area under your boat and even, with practice, to identify species of fish you see on the screen. This cannot be done with lesser locators, though the cheaper units are vastly better than nothing.

To give you an idea of how effective this sonar technology can be, consider this. Fisheries biologists use sonar devices costing many thousands of dollars to take census data of various species of fish in large lakes. If the technology can handle such a task as that, it can find you a few kokes.

Among the medium priced models you may want to look at the Bottom Line Tournament Master SF3, the Humminbird Wide Vision, or the Eagle Ultra III. These are all impressive units.

The Tournament Master SF3 is good down to 1500 feet and is GPS compatible; it sells for about $550. This unit looks both to the side and downward, with cone angles of 9 and 18 degrees respectively.

The Wide Vision is good to 1000 feet, has probably the sharpest screen in this price range, and sells for about $330. This unit has a duel beam transducer the cone angles of which are 16 degrees and 53 degrees respectively.

The Ultra III is good to 600 feet, has split screen capabilities, is a good sharp unit, and sells for about $270. This finder produces a single cone of 20 degrees.

Lowrance, Interphase, Apelco, Furuno, and several other companies also have excellent offerings. Some are video units. I think the LCDs are more practical for most anglers, as they are tougher, lighter, less expensive, and more waterproof than the videos. A video is good in a closed boat, where it stays dry, and does give you detail you cannot get otherwise.

GPS

You may wish to buy a unit that is GPS compatible, even if you do not plan to use the GPS right away. GPS, the instrumentation that uses signals from satellites to indicate your exact location and course, is wonderful. Not only will it guide you back home on large lakes, it will get you back to fishing hot spots that are hard to identify with landmarks. It can literally take you back to an unmarked spot the size of your boat.

Of course if you have a unit that is not GPS compatible, you can purchase a portable GPS unit that you can use on the lake or while out hunting or hiking. That may be an even better way to go.

Flashers

If you fish mostly shallow water or want a second unit, you might consider a flasher. Good ones are made by Zercom, Vexilar, and Humminbird. The FL-8 by Vexilar is my pick because it is easy to read, rugged, and astonishingly sensitive. In shallow water, you can literally watch a small perch take a tiny jig and predict down to the fraction of a second when the little guy is going to jiggle the rod. Flashers are at their best at depths of less than 60 feet.

Vexilar FL-8 Flasher.

Flashers can be made portable with the purchase of a kit. As such, they are great for ice fishing. They are much more resistant to cold than are the LCD units, which tend to go dormant in very cold or very hot conditions.

Portables

If you rent boats often, buy a portable kit with your locator. Instead of the suction cup transducers that come with these, I recommend the portable transducer brackets sold by Cabela's, Bass Pro Shops, and other vendors. You attach the transducer to the bracket and then clamp the bracket to the side or transom of the boat. They are more stable then those irritating suction cups. (Would that I had a $100 bill for every time I have found myself trolling my transducers because the suction cups popped off.)

Whatever you purchase in the way of a finder, by all means, get the best you can afford or justify, and take time to learn to use it well. Experiment until you can manually fine tune the sensitivity and range to your needs at the time.

Working and learning to get the most from your finder will be some of the best angling time and money you will ever spend, enhancing your angling success from then on. A good fringe benefit is that you will get to know the lake you fish better than you ever knew it before.

OTHER DEVICES

Trolling Speed Indicators

Luhr-Jensen sells a little unit called the Luhr-Speed that clamps to your gunwale and is accurate down to a tenth of a mile per hour. It was formerly marketed by another firm as the Accutrol, until Jensen bought it. As critical as trolling speed can be with kokanee, I think the Luhr-Speed should be a part of every kokanee angler's equipment collection. I have seen times when kokes would hit a lure trolled at 0.8 miles per hour and turn up their noses at the same lure trolled at 1.2 MPH, and vice versa.

MOTORS

Trolling with Gasoline Motors

Some research has been done on the effects of sound in the boat on nearby salmon by Charlie White in British Columbia with his famous underwater camera. His studies show that nothing—jumping around in the boat, dropping tackle boxes, pounding, talking loudly—has as much effect on nearby fish as do sudden changes in the sounds emitted by a gasoline motor. The smoother your gasoline motor idles the better.

Many anglers troll with large motors. Most large outboards will not troll slowly enough for kokanee unless their effectiveness is in some way inhibited. This can be done by dragging a bucket or other object of high resistance behind the boat, or with a trolling plate that negates much of the work done by the propeller. These devices may make it possible to troll at a speed of 0.8 to 1.0 MPH with a 40-horse or larger motor, but there are much better ways.

Many anglers have small "kicker" motors on their boats. This is usually a gasoline motor of 6 to 15 horsepower. One simply cruises to the fishing area with the big motor, turns it off, and starts the kicker. The idle speed is set on the small motor to provide the desired boat speed. Steering can be accomplished by leaning out and grabbing the tiller or by having the small motor tied into the main engine with a rod that causes both motors to always be facing the same direction. A good little motor like the 6 HP Johnson, to name an outstanding example, will run at slow idle all day long without hurting itself, and is fairly satisfactory as a trolling motor.

Electric Trolling Motors

I have done considerable trolling with gasoline motors, but in the last two or three years I have tried to avoid the practice. Nothing in the sport of trolling is more annoying to me than the stink of half-burned gasoline, the gurgling unsteady sound of a gasoline motor behind me as I try to concentrate on and enjoy catching fish.

Terry Wygart

Ron Carey grins with pleasure after catching a nice Flaming Gorge kokanee. Note electric downrigger. Ron is an expert kokanee and trophy brown trout angler.

Little is more satisfying than the nearly inaudible hum and odor-free operation of a sweet little electric motor.

If the fish are less than 30 feet deep, I think the quiet method is more effective. I feel I catch more fish when trolling with my Minn Kota than when trolling with a gasoline engine.

I know I have more fun with the decibel-belching carbon burner off. My preference is that the loudest noise out there be the wind across my big ears, the singing of the downrigger, the yammering of seagulls, the slap of the occasional wave, the jumping of a fish. These are delightful sounds that can increase the pleasure derived from a trip. They are seldom heard when the gasoline motor is running.

There are many good trolling motors on the market now. I am partial to Minn Kotas, but Motor Guide and several other companies are making very fine models. They are getting larger, too. There was a time when you could use electric motors only to position a boat. The term "trolling motor" was a misnomer. The electric motors would not take the punishment of long-range trolling. There are now motors capable of moving the largest fishing boats along at respectable trolling speeds for hours with no damage.

If you have a boat with a console, you may want to look carefully at the trolling motors designed to attach to the main motor, with controls at the console. Minn Kota came out with one of these in 1996. It is available in thrusts up to 96 pounds. One could nearly ski behind that behemoth, fishing rod in one hand, of course.

We rented a 24-foot pontoon boat last summer and trolled all morning with our Minn Kota. Then we pulled into a tiny side canyon and went swimming. When we got ready to go, the 55-horse motor would not start. After trying several things, we started back toward the marina powered only by the trolling motor. At full power, it carried us along at a decent clip, even with a stiff cross breeze. Fortunately, we were only about two miles from the marina, but the little Minn Kota got us back without a hitch.

If I were using a very small craft, such as the previously mentioned canoe or Porta-Bote, I would purchase only a large, beefy trolling motor. Minn Kota's "Extreme Transom" line offers thrusts up to 70 pounds. It is doubtful you could get a gasoline motor rated safe for such small craft that would perform much better.

If my boat were large, I would consider two electric motors, one fore and one aft. I would also give careful consideration to the new motors that are controlled by a remote infrared device. They can be started, stopped, steered, and the speed controlled from anywhere in the boat, even from outside it (you've no doubt seen Bill Dance stand on the dock and call his boat in from out in the lake). Other trolling motors allow you to set a course and speed and the motor will adhere to that, regardless of wind and current.

Three

FISHIN' TACKLE

You may remember the old story of the panhandler that came by a lady's house and asked if he could use her kitchen to make stone soup. He held in his hand a stone from which he said he planned to make it.

She let him come into her kitchen—now you know this was long ago—and provided him with a pan and large mixing spoon, which she placed on the stove. He put the stone in a pan, poured water over it, began to heat it. When it was hot, he said, "Now that will be delicious as it is, but it would be oh so much better with an onion."

So she brought him an onion, which he quickly peeled and cut into the water. "Now that will be very good as soon as it cooks," he said, "but it would be even better with a few potatoes." And so the routine went until into the stone soup had been added various vegetables, some macaroni, seasonings, and a large piece of beef. Finally he was satisfied and they ate the beef stew, which had long since ceased to be "stone soup."

Picking out kokanee fishing equipment is a little like making stone soup. Assuming the angler has a boat and motor and some basic fishing equipment already, he buys some kokanee lures, some lead line, snubbers, attractors. He goes out and hopefully catches a few kokanee with the rig. "This is great," says the angler, "but how much better I could do with a fish locator." After the finder comes a downrigger, then an electric trolling motor, then a lighter rod and reel, a light for night fishing, or a GPS. Soon the investment in fishing equipment equals what one might pay for, say, a fully rigged Japanese trawler. As any confirmed kokanee addict will tell you, however, such investments are negligible compared to the joy gleaned from the activity.

SIZING TACKLE TO THE FISH

Some anglers say that kokanee are primarily good for eating, not being much of a sport fish. Oh, they say, they are scrappy fighters, but not in the same league as rainbows or bass. I take issue with that.

The problem is that much of our kokanee population consists of relatively small fish that are all too often taken on heavy tackle. How can an angler feel the fight of a one-pound fish when between the angler and the fish are 70 yards of lead-core line, an ounce of lead weight, a four-foot lake troll, a six-inch snubber, and a rod that could land a 600-pound tiger shark? Kokanee do not run large, but pound for pound fight as well as anything one is likely to pull from fresh water, with the possible exception of a healthy, stream-hardened, cool water smallmouth.

I didn't realize this until about three years ago. I had been enjoying the catching of kokanee for years, doing it like most others did with big heavy equipment suitable for far larger fish. My favorite reel for this work looked like something that one would normally find mounted on the front bumper of a Jeep. I caught kokanee this way and enjoyed it. But I thought little of how well kokanee fight. I often reflected, however, on how soft their mouths are, how easily they are lost.

When I started to write this book, I had to seek out and learn from some real kokanee anglers, women and men who are innovators in the field, who have invented techniques and equipment that not only make it possible to catch more kokanee, but to have more fun doing it. In my search I ran into several accomplished anglers who opened my eyes to kokanee fishing as I now think it should be. Their ideas and experiences, filtered through the fabric of my prejudices, experiences, and opinions, make up the bulk of this book.

Though level wind reels are normally used with downriggers, good spinning and even spin-cast reels will do the job, if their drags are up to the task.

Reels

For flatlining or downrigger trolling, I like a light, high-quality level wind reel—the Shakespeare Sigma Baitcast, the Garcia S 1600-C or 3600-C, the Bass Pro Shops PQ 1000 or 2000, or the Shimano Curado, for instance. Then there is the wonderful and expensive Penn Levelmatic 920, the epitome of smooth quality.

If I want more line capacity, or if I am using lead line, I will go with the great Garcia 6500 C3, or the Penn 920, 9M, 109M, or 10. The Garcia 6500-C3 is the reel to which all level winds are compared. Penn makes, for my money, the best reels available. If Penn made small level wind reels the size of the Garcia S-3600, I would use only Penns for trolling.

Though the level winds are better for trolling, I occasionally use a high-quality spinning or spin-cast reel, one with a good drag. I have used Zebco's 33 Classic quite extensively and have found it adequate and easy to use. For an open face spinning model, I prefer the smaller Penn reels, such as the 4200 or 4300 SS, over all others. Penn's drags hold up to the stresses of being used with a downrigger.

The true test of the trolling reel comes, not in fighting the fish but in letting line out as the downrigger ball drops. You need some resistance to keep things under control, but you need smooth resistance. That is where a high-quality smooth drag and ball bearing action come in handy. When dropping the downrigger ball to its desired depth, I generally loosen the drag on the reel, decrease the pressure on the downrigger clutch, and drop the ball slowly. The line must come off the reel smoothly for this to work well. With an electric downrigger, I drop the ball at a slow speed setting.

Some reels I have used tend to grab as line is stripped off and to cause the rod to bend double. Then they release suddenly and the rod straightens with a bang and line goes everywhere. Or the grabbing of the reel causes the line to be pulled from the downrigger clip, necessitating that the whole operation be started over.

Line

Some good lines for kokanee trolling are Berkeley Trilene XT green, Ultragreen Maxima, and green Silver Thread, and Garcia's Royal Bonnyl II, an invisible brown line sold by Cabela's.

I came to appreciate Bonnyl when using it in 4-pound test for catching brook trout in ultraclear streams in the Appalachians. Line there had to be invisible, or those spooky little char just seemed to evaporate into nowhere. Bonnyl was one of the few lines that would work for this. I have 8-pound Bonnyl on two rigs.

I am experimenting with Berkeley Fire Line; I am excited about it, so far. Knot strength and abrasion resistance are excellent. Fire Line handles monofilament knots well. You don't have to carry a bottle of glue around in your pocket, as with the super strong braided lines. The low-vis "smoke" color of Fire Line passes the visibility test. The line has zero stretch and is therefore very sensitive, making it an ideal line for fishing with jigs or bait. I installed 6-pound Fire Line (equivalent mono diameter, 2-pound test) on a small ABU Garcia Black Max 1600 casting reel. The reel sits on a light, high-quality, 6.5-foot Garcia graphite spinning rod. Because of its lack of stretch, this line is sensitive. If a fish so much as coughs within10feet of my jig or bait, I feel it. I do not typically use non-stretch lines for trolling.

Many do not agree that low visibility is important in a line. One writer goes so far as to say that fish have no idea what line is and it therefore does not matter whether they see your line or not. The logic sounds good, but I wonder if the fish are aware of this reasoning. I seem to get more strikes and catch more fish with low visibility green or clear mono or Bonnyl than with the yellow, pink, or aquamarine, monofilaments I have tried. Several successful guides and anglers I know agree.

Rods

For a rod that will be good for trolling all summer long, I like a light action graphite spinning rod. Some of the real experts have rods made up from 2- or 3-weight fly rod blanks by Sage, Loomis, or Cabela's. These are the ultimate in sensitivity,

A good-quality, light action, graphite rod about 7 feet long, like the Garcia pictured above, is great for kokanee angling with downriggers. Note the low price Walker downrigger.

though such a rod is not cheap. I like my light graphite spinning rods. If made by a reputable firm, they are quite sensitive.

I like long rods for this work. I consider six and a half feet a minimum, but prefer a rod of seven or seven and a half feet. The rod must match the system I am using, however. One cannot successfully troll lead-core line with a light action rod, but such a rod is ideal when using a downrigger.

For jigging and baitfishing, I have my eye on this sweet, light action, 7-foot Cabela's Fish Eagle XML spinning rod. It, or a spinning rod built on a Sage or Cabela's 2- or 3-weight fly rod blank, will probably be my next addition to the ever-growing pot of stone soup. It's a necessity to go with that sensitive new Fire Line. After all, I once bought my wife a piano instruction book and very soon had to buy her a piano to go with it.

ATTRACTORS

Attractors are devices that, when trolled ahead of a lure, attract a fish's attention. This, it is hoped, causes the fish to come closer, where it will see and take the lure. Attractors emit vibrations and flashes of light that, it is hoped, resemble a baitfish or a school of them.

Attractors come in three basic designs, two of which are sometimes called by the same name. The word flasher is overused in fishing, standing sometimes for an electronic gadget that finds fish, occasionally for an attractor similar to a dodger but with a different action, and sometimes for an attractor that consists of from two to nine spinner blades strung on a wire and often called a lake troll or pop gear.

For this discussion, the ground rule will be that a dodger is a slab of shiny metal, while a flasher is a strip of metal much like a dodger. Instead of "dodging" back and forth, however, a flasher goes round and round. I do not use flashers of this type when fishing for kokanee.

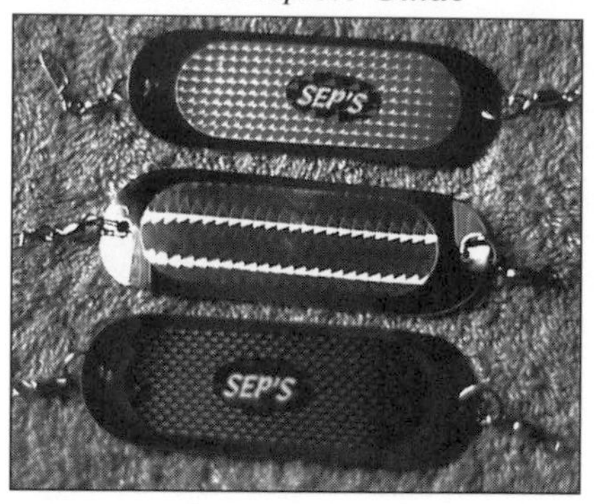

These size 0000 dodgers are examples of the type favored by the author and many others. All have a nickel finish with reflective tape on the surface.

A very good, large lake troll made by Arnie's of Colorado. Note variety of metal types and colors. Many anglers use these in-line, but they are better when attached to the downrigger ball.

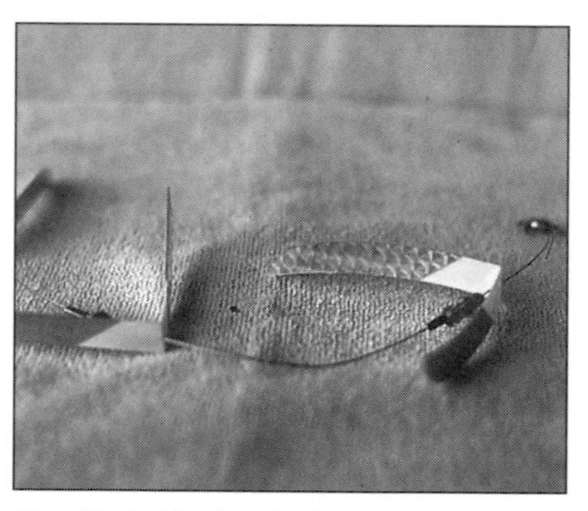

The Flash Lite by Mack' Lures of Oregon. This unique troll is virtually weightless in water and has proven highly effective in attracting aggressive kokes.

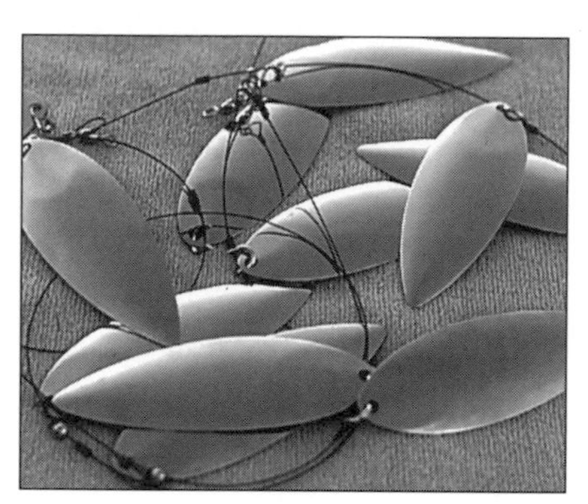

These large, high-quality trolls, sold by Vance's Tackle, are made specifically to attach to a downrigger ball or cable.

The word troll as used here is not to be confused with the ugly little varmint that lives under the bridge in certain Scandinavian folk tales. Troll as used here means a gang of spinner blades from six inches to five feet long.

Most attractors fit into one of the above categories, but not all. There are a few oddballs, many of which are very useful to the koke angler. One is a critter called a Flash Lite. Made and sold by Mack's Lures in Oregon, this device is made of a thin cable onto which curved shiny strips of Mylar are strung. It has a keel and swivels. Available in two sizes, it is an excellent attractor for trolling for most any species. The Mylar strips bend and flex and twist, showing shiny surfaces in many directions and undoubtedly getting the attention of fish in every quarter. This troll weighs next to nothing, and can be used on a light rig with very little noticeable interference. It has proven highly effective in my experiments.

I occasionally hear discussions concerning the relative effectiveness of trolls versus dodgers. I would have to say that in my experience, dodgers are more effective. There have been times when an ultralight troll would induce strikes and a dodger would not, but the reverse has been true for me most of the time. I am talking here about light equipment attached to the line, not about large trolls attached to the downrigger ball or cable.

Lake Trolls

Trolls, the gangs of spinner blades, go by several names, according to the size and the shape of the individual spinner blades. The Dave Davis, for example, generally has three large willow leaf spinner blades followed by four bear rivers, which are more rounded. Other trolls include the Beer Can, Cowbell, School-O-Minnows, Ford Fender, Doc Shelton, Little Ace, T-N-T, Dawnie, Nine Diamond, Lucky Flasher, Chug-A-Lug, and the Indiana Lake Troll. These vary in length from10 inches or so to over five feet. Blade size varies from the size of a thumbnail to larger than the palm of your hand. These devices are also referred to as "pop gear."

Most trolls come with a plastic or metal rudder near the front, as well as swivels on each end. If these items are not present, either buy other trolls or add them, as they are essential in protecting your line from twist. Luhr-Jensen sells a device that consists of a wire frame on which one can string weights. Called a "Troll Ease," it is shaped like a trolling rudder and does the job of one. By adding barrel-shaped weights, one can also use this device to control the depth at which he or she wants the gear to run.

One instance in which a rudder is not necessary is when the troll is attached to the downrigger weight or cable. Even then, the rudder does no harm. Don't take it off if you feel you may attach the troll to a fishing line later.

I have several large trolls that I use, typically attached to the downrigger ball or cable. Vance Staplin markets two excellent trolls for this purpose at a very reasonable price. They come in smooth nickel or real gold finish and are made specifically for attachment to the downrigger. I have used them in tandem with great success. Another good troll is made by Arnie's; it has both nickel and gold blades, some of which are decorated with reflective tape of various colors. Other large trolls are sold by Luhr-Jensen, a company that markets an endless array of sizes, colors and shapes. Mack's and Hildebrandt also sell some excellent trolls.

Dodgers

Dodgers are bent strips of metal with a swivel on each end. They come in a variety of finishes that is as extensive as that of trolls. Some have tape showing holographic images of baitfish on one side. Others have reflective tape of various colors, often showing a scale pattern. Dodgers range in size from about three inches long to a foot or so.

I have had the best results with small (size 0000, between three and four inches long) dodgers in nickel, preferably hammered nickel, perhaps with silver, blue, red, green, or chartreuse reflector tape on one or both sides. Over 95% of my trolling is done with a size 0000 hammered nickel dodger with silver tape on one or both sides.

Dodgers, like trolls, emit vibrations and flashes attractive to kokanee and other fish. They also add action to lures—trolling flies, for instance—that tend to be short in this area.

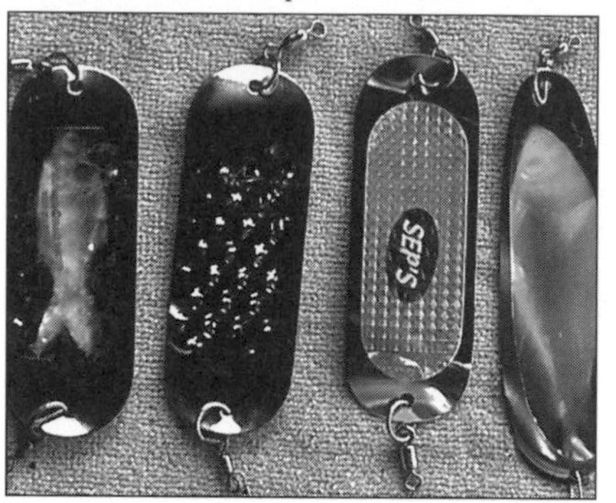

L. to R.: A hammered nickel dodger with Real Image Tape, an identical dodger without tape, a Sep's nickel dodger with chartreuse tape, and a large spoon from Real Image that serves as a very good dodger.

Ron Carey

Another fat Flaming Gorge kokanee. Note the big attractor alongside the fish.

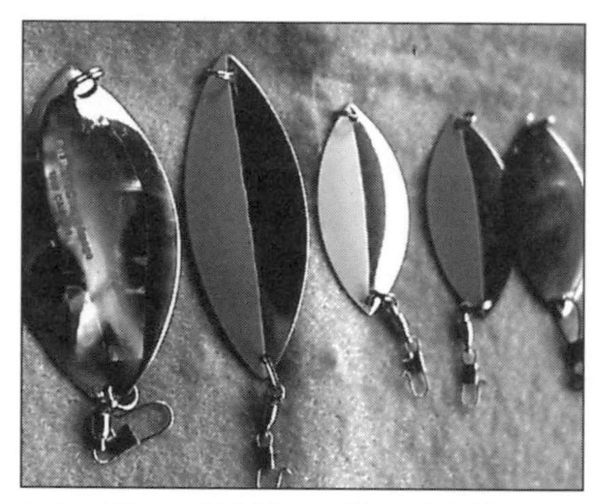

Lake Clear Wabblers. The nickel/copper model on the left has Real Image tape on it.

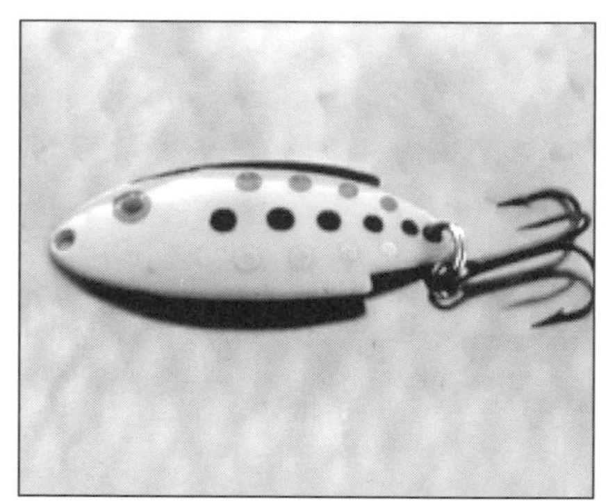

The Thomas Buoyant, a truly great kokanee and trout lure, lies atop a sheet of silver fish scale Fish Laser Tape from Real Images.

Sep's sells a dodger that glows in the dark and one in hot pink that I am anxious to try. Sep's is also marketing a nickel dodger with chartreuse reflector tape that has been dynamite for me.

Luhr-Jensen has only recently come out with a good looking line of 0000 dodgers. These are available in glow, silver plate, and various other colors and with prism tape and holograms of baitfish. It seems odd, as the two finishes are so close, but silver seems to work sometimes when nickel finish will not. Triple Teazer, now owned by Yakima Bait Company, also sells an excellent line of dodgers. Silverhorde makes some of the finest dodgers available, including the dodgers sold by several other vendors.

How necessary are attractors? That depends largely on who is advising you. Often they seem to increase the strike rate, then at other times you will do quite well by trolling just your lure. One of the top kokanee men in the country, Frank Verano of Connecticut, catches boatloads of kokanee and seldom uses attractors. There are other experts around who use them religiously, so who really knows?

Phil Johnson has a logical approach that I have adopted—I have learned so much from Phil. He frequently starts the day with just the lure, adding a dodger if strikes are few, and then adding a big troll to the downrigger ball if trolling with the dodger is not working. That way, he is always using the simplest equipment that will work on that day.

The Lake Clear Wabbler

Wabbler or wobbler, the word is a good name for this lure/attractor. It is sort of a big spoon or small dodger, depending on how you choose to use it. It is sold by Thomas M. Delaney of Gilbertsville, NY, and I like it. It comes in various sizes ranging from less than two inches long to over three. Colors range from nickel through 50/50 nickel/copper or nickel/brass through one of the metal finishes on half of the Wabbler and a bright painted finish such as chartreuse or blaze orange on the other. I like them for kokanee. I often add a patch of silver reflector tape to them.

Reflector Tape

It is a good idea to carry reflector tape in your tackle box, and to decorate your dodgers yourself. This decreases the number of expensive dodgers in which you must invest. It also adds variety and flexibility you cannot get otherwise. I buy some of my reflective tape from Luhr-Jensen, Net Craft, and Mack's.

A California company called Real Images produces some of the most innovative reflector tapes available. Some have holograms of fish on them, others sport a very real scale pattern and come in various colors. I have had the best results with the silver tape with the large scale pattern on it. Real Images also sells spoons of various sizes with their tape already attached. The larger of these make excellent dodgers, while the smaller ones are fine lures.

Reflective tape can also be used to decorate spoons, crankbaits, spinners, and other lures. This often enhances their effectiveness. Silver with some type of scale pattern seems to be most effective most of the time.

GETTING THE LURE DOWN TO THE FISH

Make no mistake, nothing that you can use to get the lure down to the fish equals a downrigger 99 percent of the time. There are situations within that remaining 1 percent when I personally prefer lead weights or spliced lead line. Even then, a downrigger, if used properly, will do the job quite well.

Downriggers cost money, and some folks simply do not have $100 or more to lay out for one. Or they may have to wait a while until they can afford a downrigger and want to fish in the mean time. Then there are times, as in the spring (or in winter in some waters), when kokes are near the surface and a downrigger is not needed to get the lure to them. Even then, however, we may need to look for a means to get our lure down to where the fish are suspended.

The Depth-O-Troll

One of the great problems encountered with devices other than downriggers is determining how deep the lure is running. We often need to know this, preferably in feet. Fish finders do not tell us the depth of the fish in colors.

Bead Tackle sells a device called the Depth-O-Troll that helps the angler determine the true depth of his lure based on the amount of line out and the angle at which the line enters the water. One simply holds the device level (there is a level on the Depth-O-Troll) with the line alongside, and reads the depth on a scale, based on the length of line out and angle of descent. The device works with divers, lead core or wire line, monofilament with weights, and even with the downrigger cable that is not hanging straight. It is one of the handiest gadgets I have encountered, especially for those who do not have downriggers.

It has two weaknesses. Since your line, once in the water, does not lie perfectly straight, but in a long curve, your lure will always be slightly less deep than the Depth-O-Troll tells you it is. Also, you need a pretty accurate feel for how much line is out. Even with these slight shortcomings, however, the Depth-O-Troll is a very handy gadget.

Diving disks like these from Big Jon can aid in getting the lure down to the kokanee or to the side of the path of the boat when fish are spooky.

Trolling Divers

Divers work by planing down into the water as they are trolled. How deeply they dive is controlled by the pitch and size of the diver, trolling speed, line thickness and other factors.

Divers are one of the least expensive ways to get your lure down to where the kokes live. Their biggest drawback, as with sinkers and lead-core line, is the difficulty of determining the depth at which one is actually trolling. They are a little more troublesome than sinkers.

Divers add action to lures that are trolled far behind the boat, as the distance from diver to lure is typically only about five feet. (Some lures, particularly crankbaits, trolled on very long lines tend to have their action dampened.) When purchased in bright colors, divers can also act as attractors.

Some divers, like the Mini Disk, Deep 'R Diver, and Dipsy Diver, can be used to draw the lure to the side of the path of the boat. This decreases running depth but widens the path of lures one is pulling through the water and separates lines and lures when several are being trolled at once. More importantly, it serves, as does a planing board, to remove the lure farther from the path of the boat when water is very clear and fish are spooky. This ability to troll away from the path of the boat can sometimes be a considerable advantage to the angler. I use divers much more often to draw my lure to the side than to get it down.

Most divers have a release that trips when a fish takes the lure. This causes them to stop planing and reduces the resistance on the line.

Lead-Core Line

More kokanee are probably caught on lead-core line than on any other device made to attain trolling depth. Lead line comes in several sizes, the most popular with kokanee anglers probably being 12- or 18-pound test. The line is made of a Dacron sheath over a lead core. The line is typically colored in 10-yard bands, so the angler can tell how much line is out. One will often hear "colors" used as a unit of measure to tell how deep kokanee are suspended. "Oh, they're down four colors today."

The trouble is that this is inexact. Four colors is 40 yards of line off the reel. The depth into which that translates is influenced by trolling speed, terminal tackle, line diameter, and "how you hold your mouth," as old anglers are fond of saying. If you aren't catching fish, it is because you "ain't holding yer mouth right." A better handle on real lure depth can be obtained by using Bead Tackle's Depth-O-Troll as mentioned earlier.

In spite of all this, thousands of kokanee come flopping into boats every year on the end of lead line. Many trout and other species are also caught this way.

If you wish to use lead line, use as light an outfit as will handle it. This translates into a medium bait casting outfit. Get a large capacity level wind reel to hold that thick line.

To rig lead core, I tie a mono leader directly to my lead line. Or, if my leader is to be short, I put a large swivel on the end of the lead core and attach a length of mono to that. To that I tie a small swivel. To this I attach a light dodger or lake troll. Then I attach a shock cord snubber and then a 2- to 3-foot leader of 8-pound mono. I attach my lure to that. If fish are not hitting, I may increase the length of the mono leader between the lead-core line and the dodger to 20 or 30 feet.

If depth is over 20 feet, I like to add a chain weight near the end of the lead line. A half ounce or an ounce of weight will greatly decrease the amount of lead line needed to get to a given depth. The shorter line enables the angler to work a school of kokanee better by making sharper turns. It also decreases tangling with lines from other boats.

Spliced Lead-Core Line

Trolling with spliced lead-core line consists of splicing in a measured length of lead core between two lengths of mono. The desired depth determines the length of lead core used. The method works best when the kokes are less than 25 feet down.

Lead Weights

Larry Federici is the superintendent of Navajo Lake State Park in northern New Mexico. He and his lovely wife, Laura, are two of the more accomplished anglers I know. In the early summer when kokanee are at a depth of about 20 to 25 feet, he likes to tie a chain weight to the end of his mono line,

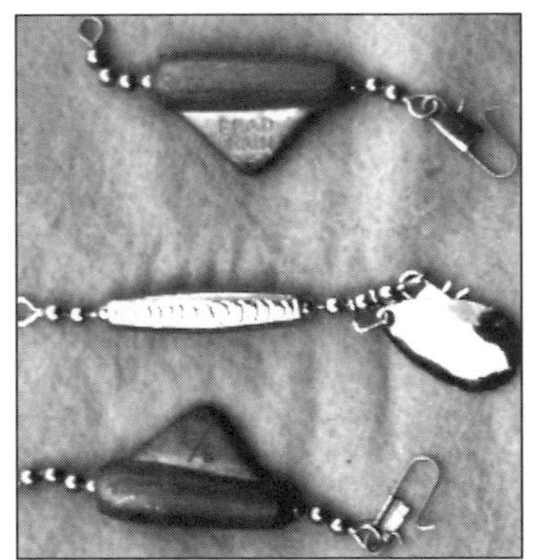

Weights from Bead Tackle. The bead-chain spinner is in the middle, with keeled trolling weights on the ends. These come in various sizes and work extremely well when kokanee are not over 25 feet deep.

then a dodger, a snubber to that, and then a couple of feet of leader, and his lure. He trolls this outfit along at a little over a mile per hour. He often jokes that as soon as kokanee hit this rig they come out of the water, giving him a chance to see his fish before he loses it. Don't let him kid you; he catches plenty.

Chain weights come in several varieties. I like those from Bead Tackle, specifically those with the spinner blade attached. With the small nickel or gold finish spinner blade the weight becomes an attractor also. They come in a diamond shape for casting and jigging and in a keeled variety for trolling.

So if you fish where kokanee don't go too awfully deep, or if you long to just fish for a day or two and not fight a downrigger, consider simply adding lead weights or a piece of lead line to your light casting outfit. They may be all you need, though you may have to do some experimenting to know the depth at which you are fishing.

Here again would be a superb application for the Bead Tackle Depth-O-Troll. One could very conveniently keep a close watch on lure depth simply by knowing the length of line out and doing a quick check.

My son Jim and I recently rented a fiberglass boat, only to find, when we got out on the lake, that my downriggers would not clamp onto the gunwales of the son of a %&$#*. It would clamp on, but would not hold onto that slippery fiberglass. We rigged up a light casting outfit consisting of a Garcia Black Max 3600, a light 7-foot Garcia graphite spinning rod and 8-pound-test green Silver Thread with a bead chain spinner and a chartreuse 1/4-oz. Thomas Buoyant spoon about three feet behind it. Copying another spoon I had lost and could not replace, I had put a patch of silver reflective tape on the side of this spoon, sort of covering the shoulder area.

We were in Utah and could not use corn, so we tipped the hook with strips of shrimp that had been soaked in a mixture of Phil Perone's Pro-Cure Herring and Anise Plus oils.

I was showing plenty of medium sized fish at 30 feet, so he put that rig in the water and let out about 100 feet of line. Almost immediately he was into a kokanee. I stopped rigging the second outfit and netted his koke, a fat 15-incher. He rebaited, sent his line back out, and was into another before I could get back to my project on the second pole. It was like that for about an hour. I never did get the other pole in the water. I didn't even get time to check his depth with the Depth-O-Troll. We had simply hit it just right.

We soon had our limits on that one pole. It had been very refreshing catching all those fish without fooling with that blasted downrigger. Sometimes simplicity, not ignorance, is bliss.

SNUBBERS

Snubbers are sections of stretchy material that reduce shock to the end of the line. Snubbers work well in situations where stretch is needed to keep a fish from tearing off the hook. They are used extensively with kokanee salmon because their mouths are very soft, because they have more than sufficient strength to tear themselves from a hook, because the attractor supplies resistance and inertia against which the kokanee can pull, and because kokanee are often caught by trolling and the shock of a normal strike is increased by the forward momentum of the boat.

Snubbers are made by several companies. Most consist of surgical tubing with a stretch line in the middle and a snap swivel on each end. A few are made from elastic or rubber bands.

Snubbers come in various lengths, and in tubing diameters from 1/8 inch (8-pound-test) to 3/8 inch (80-pound-test). Colors range from the natural amber through black, green, red, to "glo." One of the best suppliers, especially of colored and glow snubbers, is Mack's, though there are several others.

Many of the real kokanee "pros" complain that the snubber deadens their contact with the terminal tackle, or that the snubber kills the action of the lure. Greg Doering, inventor of the K-Fly, advocates putting the snubber upline of the dodger, with only line between the dodger and lure.

The "snubber" that is my favorite is not really a snubber at all but a section of shock cord used by fly fishermen to protect light tippets from breaking. The principle here is the same, a section of stretchy material that softens the shock of a muscular fish hitting your poor defenseless lure. In the case of fly fishing, the goal is usually to protect tiny, hair-thin leader material.

The shock cord, at eight inches long and only a little larger in diameter than your mono line, interferes with lure action very little, if at all. I use it exclusively for trolling, as its stretch does deaden sensitivity, just as stretchy mono is less sensitive than no-stretch line. I don't like that when I am stillfishing, where sensitivity is the name of the game.

I buy my shock cords from Feather-Craft. Each looks very much like an eight-inch section of monofilament line with a loop tied on either end. The thing is called "Item 100, The F-C Shock-Gum Section" in the Feather-Craft catalog; they sell for about a buck apiece. Feather-Craft also sells the cord in rolls.

The Shock-Gum Section is the best snubber available for my money. You hardly notice you have a snubber on. The shock-gum has less stretch than surgical tubing, but it has enough.

On infrequent occasions, I still use surgical tubing snubbers. Then I get the smallest diameter available. Of all the surgical tubing snubbers, I prefer the Mack's 1/8 inch in green or red. They have a test of 8 pounds or so, plenty of strength for kokanee. If I am trolling deep, or using a heavy in-line attractor, or lead line, I go to 3/16 inch and to the "glo" color.

Many of the experienced kokanee anglers with whom I compare notes do not use snubbers. Frank Verano doesn't. Neither does Phil Johnson. My friend Chester Bodo has quit using them. They feel that light rods, lightly set drags, properly rigged hooks, and small dodgers or trolls have done away with the need for snubbers. Given the phenomenal success of these experts, it is difficult to argue with them. Even I, bungler that I am, use them only part of the time.

But snubbers still have their place, I believe. Some experts still use them. Whether or not you use them depends on the other equipment you use and on your personal preference.

Four

THE END OF THE LINE: TERMINAL TACKLE

HOOKS

Kokanee have very soft mouths, and they are very strong fish. It's a little like Billy the Kid having had big wrists and small hands. A trick of genetics makes them hard to hold onto. More kokanee are lost by the hook pulling free from their mouths than in any other way. It is because of this that snubbers are used, as well as the lightest, most sensitive equipment that will do a given job. Hooks of the proper size and design are as important as any of this other equipment.

It seems to me that most anglers use hooks that are too small for kokanee, especially in trolling. This is partly the fault of some lure manufacturers, who should know better. They give you a good sized trolling lure, then stick a tiny single or treble hook on it that could not hold a strong healthy koke through the initial shock of the strike, let alone through the first 30 seconds of the fight.

It is a good idea to remove these pitiful hooks and install something more suitable to the size of the silvers being pursued. It is one thing to hook up with a big, mature eight-incher in, say, Spirit Lake, and quite another to take on a four-pounder at Roosevelt.

There is a flip side to this. If you get the hooks too big in the case of fluttering spoons or wobbling crankbaits, you can kill the action of the lure. While sizing hooks, you must be careful not to kill action.

Treble Hooks

Many kokanee anglers do not like treble hooks. I do. I especially like the new, wide-bite treble hooks and those that are offset a tad, causing the hook to turn as it sinks into flesh. If you buy treble hooks that are not offset, you can offset them carefully with a pair of pliers. Look at an offset treble hook and make your angles similar to theirs.

For big kokanee, 17 inches and up, I go with a size 4 treble hook, when I can get it. If necessary, I will take a 6. One style I recommend is the gold-finished treble from Mack's that has phosphorescent material molded on it. It seems to me that the glow material increases the rate of strikes. Alternately, I install Eagle Claw Laser Sharp red trebles with the gold eye. The red/gold combination seems to attract ol' br'er koke's attention too.

For smaller kokanee, size 6, 8, or even 10 treble hooks of the types described above will work admirably.

Single Hooks

As to single hooks, I recommend two kinds: the red hooks by Gamakatsu, Owner, Fenwick and, Eagle Claw commonly called Octopus, Steelhead, or Salmon Red hooks, and the Kahle style hooks made by several companies. In the red hooks, I favor Eagle Claw for the price. There is no arguing with the quality of the other brands named; they are among the best available. The Gamakatsu hooks are probably the sharpest hooks on the market, but Eagle Claw Lazer Sharp hooks are quite sharp also.

Kahle hooks are hard to find in anything but bronze finish. I finally found some size 4 Kahle hooks in nickel finish in the Off Shore catalog. I would have preferred size 6 hooks, as the wide-bite Kahle is effectively larger than a salmon hook of the same size number. While a size 2 salmon hook feels about right for big kokes, the number 4 Kahle seems awfully big. Eagle Claw should make a Kahle hook in gold/red.

I believe the Kahle holds kokanee better than any other single hook. For smaller kokanee, it may be necessary to go to size 6 or 8 in the salmon hooks, or an 8 or 10 in the Kahle.

The Double Hook Rig

Phil Johnson rigs his single hooks in a way that greatly reduces losses while playing kokanee. Phil probably lands over 95 percent of the kokanee he hooks. Few anglers achieve such statistics.

Phil snells two #2 Gamakatsu Steelhead Reds so that the eye of one is about a half inch from the bend of the other. Next he strings a single 4 or 6 mm orange, glow, or red bead on the leader ahead of the hook. He typically uses this rig on the Apex and Wee Tad lures. The koke usually strikes and hooks itself on the front hook. As the koke shakes its head while fighting, the back hook usually catches it outside the mouth on the face where the tissue is tougher, thus the salmon seldom escape. Only a good hook like a Gamakatsu is sharp enough to drive through the hard tissue on the outside of the koke's face.

A less effective but quickly rigged double hook setup can be made by cutting up a 1/8-inch diameter snubber and removing the cord from inside the surgical tubing. Take a 1/4-inch section of the tubing and slip it over the eye of a Siwash or other large-eyed hook. It helps in slipping on the tubing if you wet the eye of the hook with saliva. Now wet your primary hook with saliva and run the primary hook through the tubing section so that it passes through the eye of the second hook. Bring this stinger hook around toward the back of the bend of the first hook; thus it will not interfere with the bite of the first hook.

A variation on this stinger hook quick fix theme is to run the big end of a small Duolock Snap though the eye of your proposed stinger hook and close it, then put your piece of surgical tubing over the small end of the Duolock snap and run the first hook through that. This allows a tad more freedom for the stinger hook to move around and allows you more choice in stinger hooks, including red hooks, Kahle hooks, and trebles that have small eyes.

COLOR

The Electromagnetic Spectrum

The following explanation is vastly oversimplified. That is not in deference to your lack of ability to understand, but to my lack of understanding. To talk about light in scientific terms requires math that I am unable to handle. When you start to dwell on massless particles and wave functions, things grow hazy in a hurry.

Visible light is but a small portion of a vast array of different frequencies or wavelengths of a form of energy called electromagnetic radiation. Electromagnetic radiation travels through a vacuum at a velocity of approximately 186,000 miles per second. It occurs in the form of very small massless particles called photons. Each photon has its own wave length or frequency. The shorter the wavelength (or the higher the frequency), the more energy that photon contains. The whole array of these wavelengths from the shortest to the longest is called the electromagnetic spectrum.

At the short end of the spectrum are cosmic and gamma rays. So powerful are these rays, that they are extremely lethal to living organisms. Moving across the spectrum from shorter to longer wavelengths, we encounter x-rays, ultraviolet radiation, visible light, infrared waves, microwaves, and radio waves.

The ultraviolet region causes suntan, sunburn, and skin cancer. It, like x-, gamma, and cosmic rays, is lethal in all but the smallest doses to most organisms, though it is not nearly so powerful as those other three. It is often used to kill disease germs in water. If it were not for our atmosphere's ozone layer, which absorbs much of the UV radiation from the sun, ultraviolet radiation would put an end to life as we know it.

The visible light portion of the spectrum ranges in wavelength from about 380 nanometers (a nanometer, abbreviated nm, is a billionth of a meter) to 750 nm. Specifically, we see light in the 380 nm area as deep violet, 400 nm as violet, wavelengths around 450 as blue, 500 as green, 550 as yellow, 600 as orange, 650 as red, and 700 to 750 as various shades of dark red. Beyond 750 nm, light is again invisible to us, though our skin can sense some wavelengths as what we call radiant heat.

Going up in wavelength, down in power, from visible are infrared, microwaves, and radio waves. Some frequencies in all these classes have been put to use by man, primarily for communication, radar, and cooking baked potatoes. But back to visible light.

The colors we "see" are not properties of the light itself, but are supplied by our brains as interpretations of the reactions of the retinas in our eyes to the various wavelengths. All the visible wavelengths, and many that are invisible, are contained in white sunlight.

Water affects light by refracting and absorbing it. To refract a beam of light means to bend it. Absorbing light means that the molecule of water or some substance contained therein actually absorbs the energy of the particle of light. That energy usually then results in a rise in temperature of the water.

The water's ability to influence light varies with the wavelength of the light and with the clarity of the water. Within the visible spectrum, red light is absorbed more readily by water than is orange. Objects that reflect red light are thus robbed of their color more quickly under water than are orange objects. This trend continues to green and blue, which are influenced least of all visible wavelengths. Purple and violet, although they have shorter wavelengths, are affected more than are blue and green.

As one drops deeper in water, the color associated with the longest visible wavelength, red, turns black below about 20 feet, and is already getting a little drab at 10. Orange lasts a little deeper and yellow a little deeper still. Yellow appears as light gray at 45 feet. Green and blue are only slightly affected at 50 feet, and maintain their color much deeper.

Thus in regular finishes, blue or green lures and dodgers are more readily seen, attract more attention, in deep water than do lures in red or orange.

Fluorescence

A non-fluorescent red object must be hit with red light (contained in the sun's white light) in order to appear red to our eyes. A fluorescent red object will appear red, even if hit by light of another wavelength, such as blue or green. Fluorescent objects thus maintain their color to much greater depths than do their non-fluorescent counterparts.

If you were trolling two lures at a depth of 60 feet, for instance, one of non-fluorescent bright red, and the other of fluorescent red, the lure with the non-fluorescent finish would appear gray or black and would not stand out from its background. The fluorescent lure, being hit at that depth by plenty of green and blue light, would appear bright red and would induce more strikes from red-loving kokanee. But there is a catch that we will discuss later.

Fluorescent finishes and dyes are available in lures, yarns, and dodgers of many colors and are powerful tools for the angler. As more and more lures and dodgers become available in these finishes, the wise angler will stock some in his tackle box. Now for the catch. You may draw the conclusion from this that you can get all fluorescent finished lures and forget about the effects of water depth on color. BEEEP! You lose. Thank you for playing.

As the red light leaves the fluorescent red lure, it travels through the water. Being red, it shifts quickly to brown, then black. At a longer distance, even the fluorescent lure looks black or gray.

If the water is clear, a fish may see your lure at some distance when it appears dark and swim toward it, attracted by motion, vibration, or plain curiosity. As the fish draws near, it will see the lure undergo a sudden color shift from gray to bright red. It may not be prepared for this surprise. This shift at such close range may very well scare the poor little sucker into not striking.

Beware of fluorescent lures in readily shifted colors (red, orange, violet, indigo) in clear water. These colors are most useful in more turbid waters where the lure cannot be seen at a long distance.

The color that is most visible at long distance in deep water seems to be fluorescent chartreuse. It is a pretty good bet in any water due to its visibility and to the lack of that sudden, close range shift.

Phosphorescence

Whereas fluorescent finishes emit visible light of a specific color only so long as visible light of any wavelength is hitting them, phosphorescent finishes store up the energy of light that hits them. They do this by undergoing chemical changes while the light is shining on them. When the light source is removed, these materials continue to emit visible light for a while as those chemical changes reverse and release their stored energy.

Phosphorescent finishes are commonly identified as luminescent, glow or "glo." Lures and dodgers with these finishes are increasingly effective as water depth

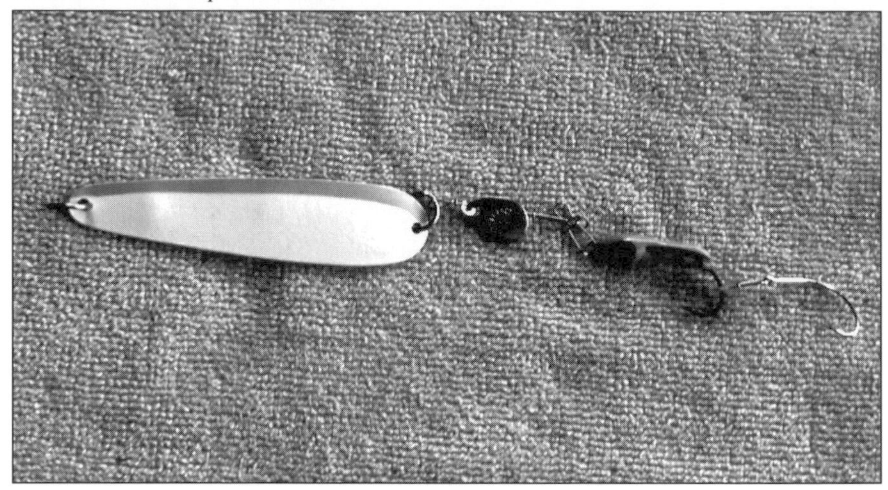

A Vance's Bug in tandem behind a Luhr-Jensen Flutter Spoon. Both these lures are phosphorescent, making them highly effective in deep water or in lakes with poor visibility.

increases. They are also dynamite at night. The night angler should remember that glow finishes need to be reactivated periodically with a source of bright light. Camera strobes work well for this. This recharging of your lure's phosphorescent properties is essential, even on bright sunny days. Shoot them at close range with a strobe even when the sun is shining.

A good example of the effectiveness of glow material is the phenomenal Vance's Bug, made by Vance Staplin in California. This is one of the most deadly kokanee lures to come along in years, but the Bug does not work as well on bright spring days when kokanee are10 feet down. Why? The bug is a killer partly because it glows in the dark. To function at its best, it needs to be in low light conditions—early morning, late evening, night, down beyond about 30 feet, or in turbid water, where it can stand out from the background.

Another effective glowing lure must be homemade. Certain specialty stores—Miller's Outpost is one—sell small images of the moon and stars for folks to stick on their bedroom ceilings. They are called "astral lights"; if you can find them, get the ones made in Newberry, Connecticut. These are made of plastic sheeting and can be cut into any shape you want. If you take a leader with a two-hook rig on the end, string on four or five beads and then string on a willow leaf or guitar pick shaped piece of this glow plastic into which two holes have been punched near the ends, you have made a very effective lure. Shoot it with the strobe and fish it like an Apex lure or a wedding ring spinner. The curved plastic has little action, but Phil Johnson and other anglers have had phenomenal success with it in late summer when kokes are deep.

Many other lures are available in phosphorescent finishes. Prime examples are Yakima Bait's Flatfish and Vibric Rooster Tail and several of the lures from Mack's. Sep's and Luhr-Jensen sell herring dodgers that glow in the dark, and Jensen has its Needlefish and Flutter Spoon in glow finishes. The phenomenal little Bingo Bug, made by Frisky Plastics and sold by Shasta Tackle, is made in glow models. With its Flatfish-like shape and action, it is a killer.

Metal Finishes

As one goes deeper into the water, nickel, chrome, and silver finishes remain essentially unaffected. Brass tends to shift to a pale yellow at great depth, whereas copper looks light gray.

TROLLING LURES

One of the great mysteries of this sport is why kokanee hit lures at all. It is a well-known fact that kokanee are eaters of plankton. They do, on occasion, take adult and young insects. I have been able to find no evidence whatsoever that kokanee eat fish, though some biologists claim they do. Yet drag a minnow-imitating lure by a kokanee and it will often slam it. My guess is that this behavior has to do with the defense of some territory, perhaps a territory that moves with the fish or the school.

Perhaps this is one of those occasions on which one should count blessings and not look the proverbial gift fish in the mouth. I rejoice in the fact that they do hit lures, for it has given me many hours of unforgettable angling enjoyment.

One thing is true: many tackle makers think of kokanee as small fish, as well they are in many lakes. Many lures you see designed for kokanee consist of tiny spinners with little #2 blades and #8 single hooks. These are ideal for the little kokes in Bullard's Bar in California, but the bruisers in Roosevelt, Deer, Loon, Hauser, Holter, Strawberry, Don Pedro, Flaming Gorge, and Eleven Mile will be insulted by these little trinkets. They may be inclined to send such tackle back to its owner in little pieces and swim away laughing.

So some companies have begun making larger tackle suitable for kokanee. The Jim Diamond with the #6 Kahle hook is a step in the right direction, being larger than Mack's Kokanee Killer. Mack's largest Super Wedding Ring and Double Whammy wedding ring lures are larger still, and are suitable for a kokanee of over two pounds.

Spoons

For the sake of discussion, let's divide kokanee trolling lures into five classes: spoons, spinners, wedding ring spinners, crankbaits, and trolling flies.

Some of the more effective kokanee trolling spoons include the Thomas Buoyant, Z-Ray, Mack's Imperial Magic, Needlefish, Willospoon, Tasmanian Devil, Cripp, Humdinger, Sep's Secret, Sep's Kokanee Kandy, Dick Nite, Phoebe, Little Cleo, Thunder Lures Bang-O-Bugs, Mack's Dynamic, and the Triple Teaser. A Canadian lure called the Deadly Dick that resembles the Kastmaster is also quite effective.

The Needlefish comes in an immense variety of colors from plain silver to glow. The rainbow pattern is called the "Kokanee Special." I like the new "Hot Tail" colors with that tiny spinner blade near the hook. The nickel/red is a killer. I am fond of the "Glo/Fluorescent Green Stripe" pattern in the Needlefish, the Flutter Spoon, and the Luhr-Jensen size 0000 Dodger for deep, late summer trolling.

Another very productive spoon is the Triple Teaser. Like the Needlefish, the trolling weight Teaser (there is a casting weight that is heavier) is light and given to a fluttering motion, probably much of the secret of its success. I have had many anglers come to me praising the effectiveness of the Teaser in hammered silver

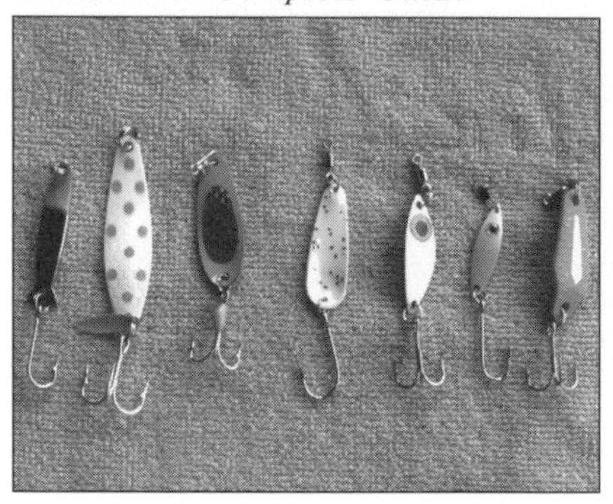

Kokanee spoons. L. to R.: Kokanee King, Needlefish, Sep's Secret, Dick Nite, Willospoon, Sep's Kokanee Kandy, and Mack's Imperial Magic.

The Phoebe, by Acme, is very good for trout and kokanee. Here are four color versions.

Triple Teasers. The second from the top has a size 0 Needlefish attached to it, the one below has a Sep's Kokanee Kandy.

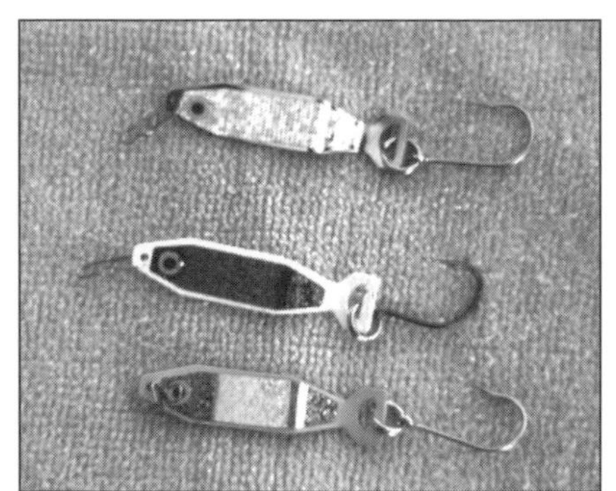

The Hum Dinger by Shasta Tackle is just that. Here are three of the many colors available in this excellent lure.

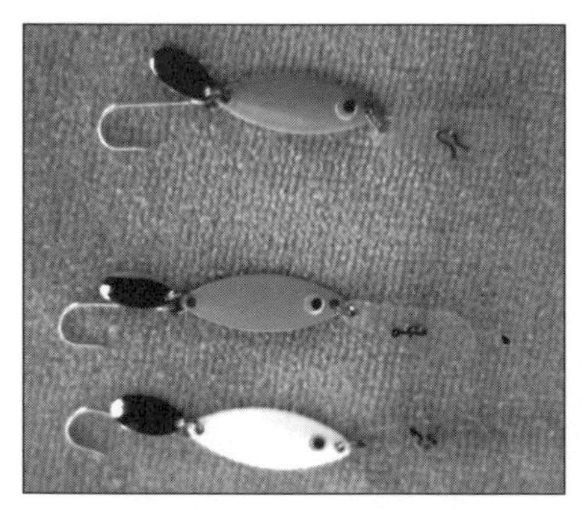

Another goodie, the Bang-O-Bug by Thunder Lures.

The first two spoons are Little Cleos by Acme. The third, with glow hook added, is covered with sparkle coating and can be bought at Wal-mart.

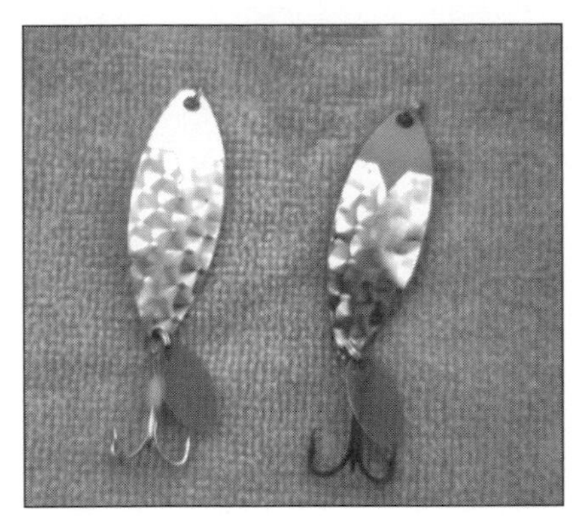

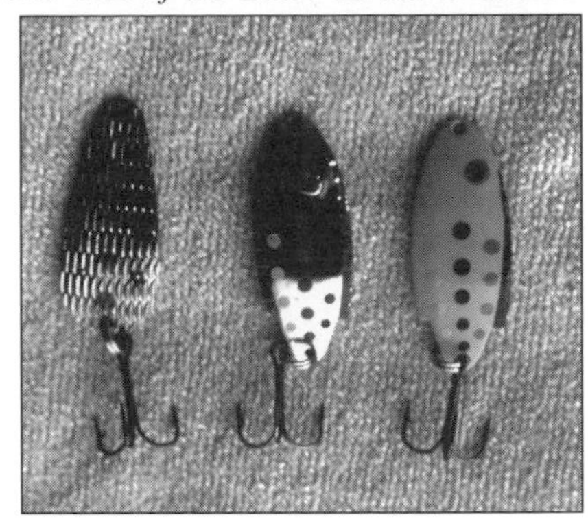

Left: *The mystery spoons by YNT Tackle purchased by the author in Kalispell, MT. These are deadly. If anyone knows where to buy these, let me know.* Right: *Two Thomas Buoyants and a Thomas Cyclone.*

with the red head. Red/white, pink/white, red/chartreuse, and orange/chartreuse are also great, as are several of the models with reflective tape on the side. On cloudy or windy days, try some of the hammered or smooth brass or copper models.

The Acme Phoebe lure comes highly recommended. This little critter is my first choice among spoons for trout, followed closely by its brother the Kastmaster. I fell in love with Phoebes decades ago, when as a college student I fished Utah's Starvation Reservoir on days off. Starvation is now more of a walleye lake, but in those days it was hot with big, very colorful, firm-fleshed rainbows. Those bows would almost always fall for a plain brass Phoebe. I have recently found the Phoebe and Kastmaster to be effective kokanee lures. Try them in rainbow trout, fire tiger, orange/yellow, blue/nickel, green/nickel, and something called "CDY" in the catalog.

The Thomas Buoyant spoon, another spoon that, like the Teaser and the Phoebe, is shaped like a small fish, is a deadly kokanee lure. Try the 1/4 ounce in bright orange. Chartreuse is good too. This lure comes in several metallic and sparkle finishes that are effective.

Dick Nite spoons are excellent, both by themselves and as half of a tandem rig with a Needlefish. Try brass/red, nickel/red, and pink sparkle. This light little spoon has excellent action.

The Jiglo spoon by Fox Creek Lures is deadly, as are the Cripp and Humdinger by Shasta Tackle. Cripps and Humdingers have what Gary Miralles of Shasta Tackle calls a "sonic chamber" that makes them quite noisy, increasing their effectiveness.

The Spin-A-Lure by (who else?) Spin-A-Lure Manufacturing reminds one of a Z-Ray. Krocodile and the Pixee spoons work quite well on kokanee, also.

Spinners

The Arnie's Vibrator Spinners have proven to be deadly on kokanee. The Arnie's is an in-line spinner, mounted on a wire body. It comes in brass and nickel with various colors of reflective tape on the blade. It is much like a Panther Martin or a Vibric Rooster Tail.

The kokanee spinner designed by Frank Verano of Connecticut is effective. This

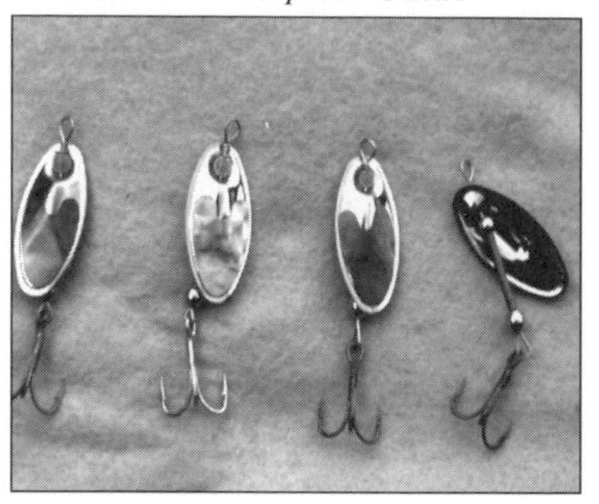

Arnie's Vibrator Spinner.

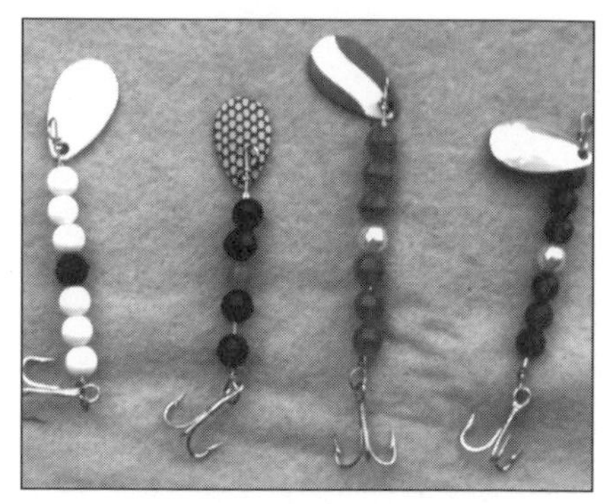

Spinners by Frank Verano.

L. to R.: Vibric Rooster Tails in fluorescent pink, luminous green (luminous=phosphorescent), silver/chartreuse Mylar. Sonic Rooster Tail in brass/flame Mylar. All these lures are from Yakima Bait.

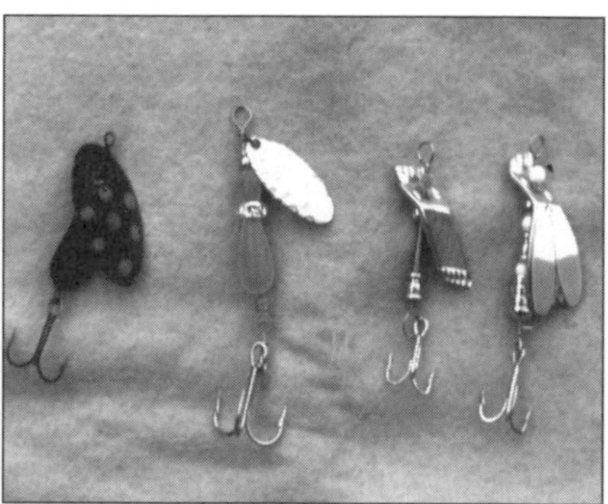

L. to R.: Panther Martin, Jeweled Alge by Mack's, Stinger and Wraith by Fox Creek.

spinner has a long wire body onto which are strung several plastic beads of various colors. This lure comes in a number of color combinations.

Frank feels that the secret of these spinners lies in the beads. A kokanee fisherman and guide for 30 years, Frank says he frequently takes kokanee with just the beads strung on the wire with no spinner blade.

Another highly effective spinner is the Mack's Jeweled Alge. The Blue Fox Vibrax is a hot item with kokanee also.

I have come to place Yakima Bait's Vibric Rooster Tail very near the top of my kokanee spinner list. It has an in-line blade like the Panther Martin and the Arnie's Vibrator Spinner and comes in a variety of bright colors appealing to kokanee and kokanee anglers.

The Wraith and Stinger spinners by Fox Creek Lures are effective, as are the Fox Creek spoons. Fox Creek is a small company in southern Colorado.

Most or all of the popular trout spinners such as the various Mepps and Panther Martins work quite well for kokanee. The Deluxe models in silver and gold are especially good. If you have some trout spinners, by all means put some corn on the hooks and give them a try.

Wedding Ring Spinners

True wedding ring spinners are a series of beads, the middle one of which is a wedding ring, and one or more spinner blades strung on a piece of monofilament line. The line is usually from 18 to 24 inches in length. One or more hooks (or a "glo" fly) are attached to the end, and may be single or treble. The hooks may be adorned with a piece of phosphorescent plastic.

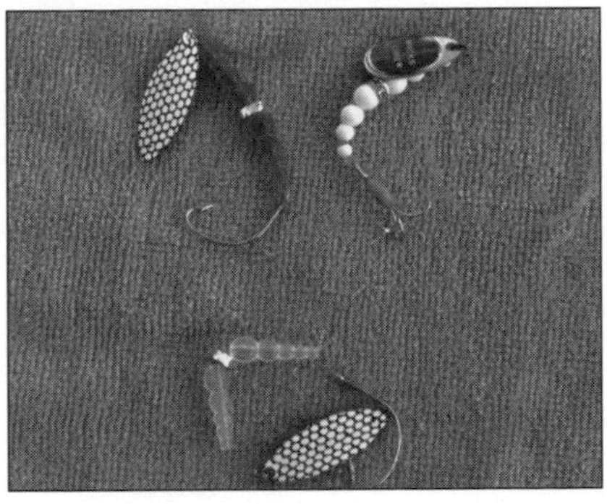

Mack's Wedding Ring Spinners, possibly the most consistently effective class of kokanee lures ever. The two with the chartreuse/scale blades are Jim Diamonds.

The wedding ring spinners as a group are some of the most consistently producing kokanee lures available. Most are produced by Mack's Lure, Inc. Mack's leads the field in wedding ring spinners and in Glo Hooks, both important tools in catching kokanee.

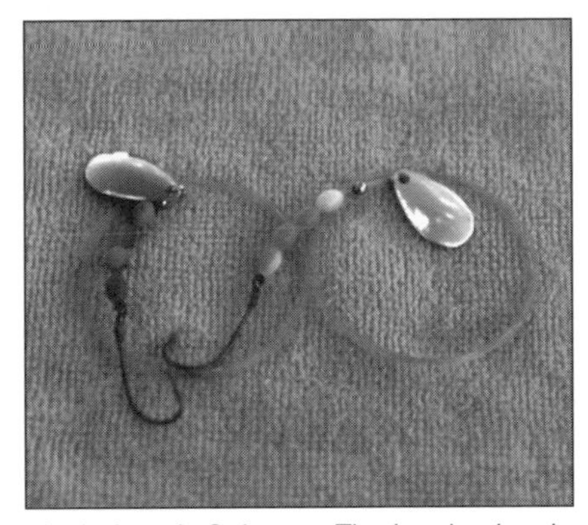

Uncle Larry's Spinners. The bands glow in the dark.

I personally prefer the Jim Diamond Spinner over most other wedding rings. The Jim Diamond sports a willow leaf blade in nickel, brass, or chartreuse or red with black scale pattern. Designed by Ron Raiha, owner of Pend Oreille Sports Shop in Sandpoint, Idaho, it has several good ideas incorporated into it. It is a tad larger than the Kokanee Killer and similar lures. The monofilament on which it is strung is longer than that on most similar lures, a good 24 inches. You can hook the Jim Diamond right to your snubber or dodger and have the lure trailing the dodger by a workable distance. This lure sports a Kahle style hook in size 6, 8, or 10. I like the chartreuse/scale blade best.

The Jim Diamond is also excellent for use with the K-Fly, Fire fly, Vance's Bug, Sep's "Bite Me" Bug, Bingo Bug, or other trolling flies. (Mack's recently told me they have quit making the Jim Diamond.)

Where kokanee run large, try the Mack's Super Wedding Ring Spinner, Double Whammy, or Double Whammy Treble wedding ring spinners. The blades on these lures are large, wide, #4 Colorado style, and come in hammered nickel or brass as well as in several painted colors.

There are many other wedding ring spinners, most made by Mack's. One spinner that fits roughly into this class has no wedding ring, but is strung on monofilament line. It is made by Uncle Larry's Lures of Sacramento, and consists of a small spinner blade, a row of four glow beads, and a single size 4 or 6 hook. It comes in several colors, and looks good. This spinner should be a real hellion if one replaces the hook with a Vance's Bug.

You can buy in-line blades from Netcraft for a decent price (Item #IA10R7).

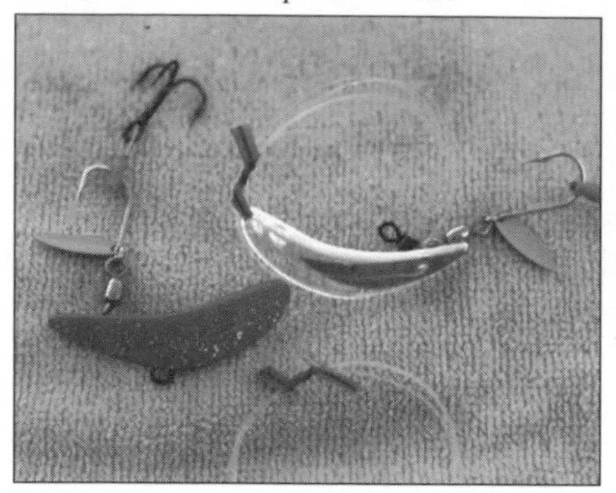

Apex Trout Killers rigged with treble stingers on original hooks.

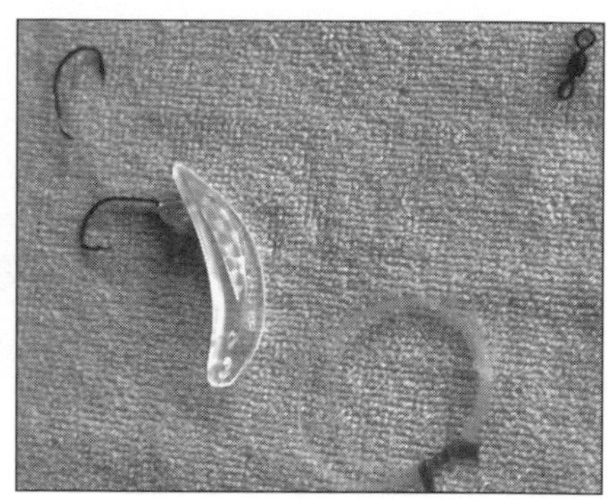

Apex Trout Killer with double hook rig. Note bead between hooks and lure.

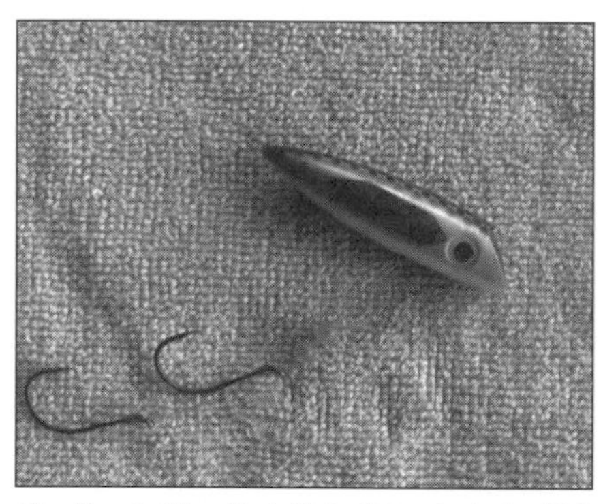

The Tomic Wee Tad. Note 2-hook rig by Phil Johnson.

This Tackle Tamer from Netcraft is a good way to store lures with leaders attached in your tackle box.

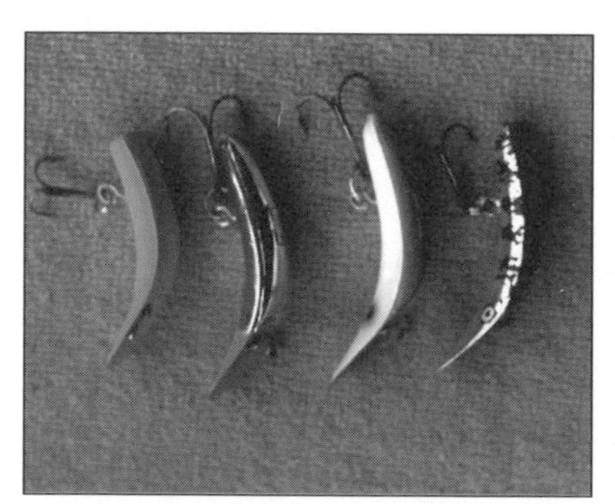

L. to R.: Jensen Kwikfish, Kwikfish with glow finish, silver/fluorescent red Flatfish, and a fluorescent pink Flatfish. These lures work well trolled slowly where kokanee are large.

L. to R.: Small Rattletrap, Jensen Rippletail, Tasmanian Devil, and Jensen Crazy Lure. The last three lie on the border between spoons and crankbaits, but are effective, as is the "Trap."

They come in sizes 0 through 6. Netcraft also has small pieces of reflective tape cut to fit a spinner blade. With these, some beads, hooks, and wire or monofilament for a shaft, you can put together some effective lures.

Crankbaits

Late in my research for this book, and following the publication of an article on kokanee in *Western Angler* magazine, I got a call from a very unusual angler, whom I have already mentioned. His name is Phil Johnson. He is retired, but works occasionally at a bait and tackle business in Merced, California, where he lives. He fishes for kokanee over 100 days per year. The poor guy. Several conversations with Phil convinced me that he is as knowledgeable about catching kokanee as anyone I have ever met.

Phil has done considerable thorough and systematic research into fishing techniques and equipment. His approach is scientific, his records complete and accurate.

Phil is the one who introduced me to the lure I now deem, overall, one of the more effective of all kokanee lures. The lure is called the Apex Trout Killer. It is made by Hot Spot Fishing & Lures Ltd. of British Columbia. The best place to order one is Cabela's or a company called Scotty's, the U.S. outlet for the Apex. Cabela's has the better prices; Scotty the larger selection.

The Apex roughly resembles a Flatfish. Instead of tying into a metal ring in the front of the lure as with the Flatfish, however, the line runs through three holes in the Apex, and ties onto a swivel that is attached to a single hook at the back of the lure. A small, bright orange metal flipper is attached to the eye of the hook. Phil removes this rig and replaces it with two red #2 Gamakatsu hooks snelled in tandem, as previously described. A single orange, glow, or red bead is placed between the front hook and the lure. The tandem hooks are tied so that the eye of the back hook is about half an inch behind the bend of the front one. The leader is left two to five feet long and averages between three and four.

Phil's other favorite kokanee lure is the Wee Tad. This little animal roughly resembles the Luhr-Jensen J-plug. It is about two inches long. As with the Apex, the line runs through the lure and ties into a swivel ahead of the hook or into the hook itself. The lure has two holes through which you can put your line. Phil feels the front hole gives the best action for kokanee. The Wee Tad is decorated with reflector tape along the sides. It is made by Tomic Lures in British Columbia. Phil rigs this lure as he does the Apex.

A variation Phil has been working with on the Wee Tad is to tie the line that runs through the lure to a swivel. There is the usual bead between Wee Tad and swivel. A leader is then rigged with Phil's standard two-hook red Gamakatsu rig, but several faceted glass beads—the resulting bead string is about an inch long—are strung on the leader ahead of the hooks. The leader is then attached to the swivel so that the hooks ride about a foot behind the Wee Tad. So far, this rig has proven very effective.

Phil, who knows far too much about salmon to be taken lightly, swears by these two lures and fishes with them in various color combinations most of the time. It harms neither the credibility of the Apex nor Phil to know that the world-record kokanee fell to an Apex.

I have used the Apex and Wee Tad quite a bit. They are great lures.

Other crankbaits I have found effective include the Rapala, Rebel, and similar minnow imitations, the Flatfish and Kwikfish, the Rattle Trap and Rattlin' Rap, the Hot Shot, and the Wee Wart, all in the smaller sizes. One can often enhance the performance of these plugs by adding scents, reflector tape, or bait.

One advantage the Apex may have over the Flatfish is the fact that it runs freely up and down the line, whereas the Flatfish does not. Theoretically, this could allow a kokanee to use the Flatfish as leverage to pull the hook from its mouth. I have lost few kokanee hooked on Flatfish, however.

Spinners with K-Flies. Left: Rooster Tail Lite with K-Fly. Middle and right: K-Flies attached to Arnie's spinners.

Trolling Flies

Trolling flies are quickly gaining in popularity. Mack's, Sep's, and other companies are marketing excellent trolling flies. Many are quite effective. Some are made of or contain glow plastic; most are brightly colored and display a lot of sparkle. Sep's flies have prominent eyes and are colorful.

A notable trolling fly designed specifically for kokanee is the K-Fly. This fly was designed and is sold by Dr. Greg Doering of Spokane, Washington. Crawdad's Bait and Tackle in Spokane is a good place to order them.

Dr. Doering is recognized widely as one of the best kokanee anglers on Franklin D. Roosevelt Reservoir, the giant body of water on the Columbia River that is one of the top kokanee lakes in the country. Roosevelt's Kokanee have suffered recently from lake drawdown associated with the anadromous salmon progress.

The K-Fly is quite beautiful, even to a human. I nearly took a bite out of the first one I unwrapped. They come wrapped individually, and the back of the pack tells of Greg's creative ways of rigging them.

The K-Fly is an effective lure in its own right. It is often made more effective by attaching it to another lure. One way is to replace the hook on a wedding ring spinner with a K-Fly.

I set up my first K-Fly rig with a Jim Diamond. The K-Fly was chartreuse with a red yarn beard and chartreuse/bluegreen sparkle tail and wings. The wings and tail are stiff, designed to produce a finny, swimming motion as the fly is pulled through the water. One should push or fluff these stiff wings forward before putting the fly in the water. The fly sports a single hook and a treble trailer. The Jim Diamond I chose for this had red beads and a red blade with black scale pattern.

I trolled this rig two feet behind a 0000 dodger, baiting the single hook with two grains of white corn. I couldn't keep the kokanee off the darned thing! I rigged another with a chartreuse/black blade, orange beads, and a K-Fly that was primarily orange and red. It is just as effective. This combo is one of the more consistently productive lures I have tried, and has become one of my favorites.

After I became acquainted with Vance Staplin and his Vance's Bug lure, I attached some of those bright little Bugs to Jim Diamonds, Kokanee Killers, Double Whammys, and other similar spinner combinations. If kokanee are more than 30 feet down, or if light is otherwise poor, this rig is a real killer. I have been using a Mack's Glo or Eagle Claw red/gold treble stinger on the Bug, attaching it with a small Duo Lock snap and a piece of rubber tubing as described elsewhere.

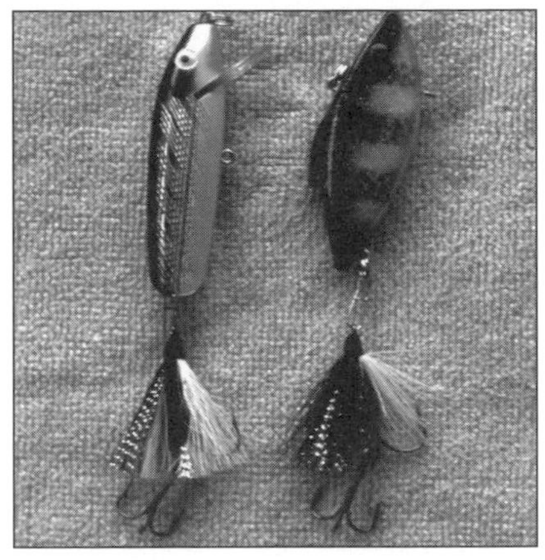

Crankbaits and K-Flies. Top, front half of a jointed Rebel. Bottom, Rattletrap.

Phil Johnson said that the Bug is one of the only lures he has ever seen outfish the Apex. Vance Staplin, who is selling this critter, is a successful kokanee angler and guide.

All these flies can be used without the wedding ring spinners, though I think they are at their best in combination with some type of other lure. I cut the hook off an Arnie's Vibrator Spinner and replace it with a small Duolock Snap, to which I can then attach a K-Fly or Vance's Bug. This has proven to be an effective combination.

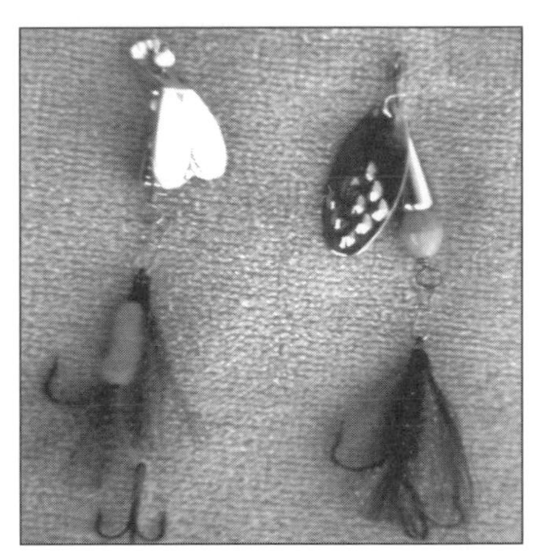

Mack's Pandana Glo Spinner (top) and a Fox Creek Wraith with K-Flies attached.

A similar hot item is a Rooster Tail Lite spinner with a K-Fly or the Bug behind it in place of the treble hook. *The Outdoor Press* recently announced that an angler on Roosevelt took a 4-pound, 23-inch kokanee on a wedding ring spinner with a K-Fly behind it. That angler said he also had good success with the Rooster Lite/K-Fly combination. Another good combo is either the K-Fly or the Vance's bug combined with the Vibric Rooster Tail. I rig by cutting off the hook and replacing it with a small Duo-Lock snap.

An even more unusual combination is the K-Fly attached to the front part of a jointed crankbait. Some anglers are having great success with this. Now Dr. Doering has come out with the K-Fly Tail, a version of the K-Fly designed to replace the rear half of a jointed Rapala or Rebel.

The rear half of the crankbait, usually a size J-9 Rapala or J-10 Rebel in silver color, is removed and replaced directly (no leader, just a split ring or Duolock) with the K-Fly Tail. The hook is removed from the belly of the crankbait half. This combo is trolled very slowly to give an enticing back and forth swimming action. The big kokanee of FDR are eating it up; there is no reason to think that large kokanee anywhere else will not do likewise.

Five

BAIT

BAIT KOKES LIKE

Some of the best kokanee fishermen I know swear you will catch more kokanee with bait on the lure; others of equal knowledge say it is unnecessary. Me? I think bait increases strike frequency. Furthermore, some baits increase it more than others. I suggest you conduct your own experiments, draw your own conclusions.

So what bait would a kokanee like? Zooplankton? Do you string *Daphnia* on a hook with a forceps, using a powerful hand lens or portable microscope for adequate resolution? That is, after all, their preferred food. Fortunately, there are more convenient baits that attract kokanee, though no one has a clue as to why.

The most popular baits are maggots, pieces of earthworm, and corn. Power Bait, marshmallows, pieces of shrimp, and salmon eggs are used also, though maggots and corn are typically more productive. Worms are so-so in spring and early summer, less effective later, and tend to attract rough fish like trout.

Maggots

Maggots of various sizes and colors are effective, but can be hard to obtain. Some folks do not care for handling maggots, though commercially raised maggots are not really dirty. The problem lies more with the name than the creature. The word "maggot" does tend to conjure up memories of less than pleasant sights and smells. Perhaps that is why the bait companies have come up with names like poppers (big maggots), spikes (regular maggots) and best of all, Eurolarvae (colorfully dyed maggots).

Spikes are convenient to keep; refrigerated, they will live quietly for weeks. Follow the supplier's directions on poppers and Eurolarvae. Spikes can be purchased from Nature's Way. Poppers and Eurolarvae can be ordered from Vado's Express Bait.

Maggots are available at many bait shops in Montana and in the Northwest, but are not readily available from Utah south. However you get your hands on them, maggots are decent kokanee bait.

As to which to purchase, I have had success with all of them, though I slightly favor the Eurolarvae. If colored hooks can make a difference, it is reasonable that a colored larva may.

Corn

Canned corn, particularly scented corn of the correct variety, may be the best kokanee bait of all, but it is illegal in some areas. Green Giant White Shoepeg

Bob Beach

Eurolarvae, or colored maggots, can be quite effective as kokanee bait.

appears to be more effective as a kokanee bait than yellow corn, though yellow corn of any brand will catch them. You may have to ask your grocer to order you a case of Jolly Green Giant white Shoepeg, as it is not always on the shelf.

The white Shoepeg seems to bleed more flavor and scent into the water than do other varieties. It is tough and stays on the hook well when trolled, also.

Phil Johnson first called my attention to the significance of the way one puts corn on a hook. Like Phil, I now typically bait with two grains, placing them parallel on the hook, flat sides together, with the hook through the thick end of each grain. I position the grains to ride right on the bend of the hook. This way, the grains, it seems to me, sort of wave as the lure is trolled, adding a minute amount of additional motion that may be attractive to the koke.

If I have two hooks, I may put two grains on the main hook and one on the trailer. Occasionally I put one grain only on each. If I am not getting a good response from the fishes, I put two grains on each hook. For trebles, I typically put a grain on each branch, but that too may vary, as the mood of the kokanee dictates.

Green Giant Shoepeg corn, Pro-Cure Scents, and plastic containers used to combine them into the best of kokanee baits.

Power Bait

Power Bait, Power Wigglers and salmon eggs are fairly effective on occasion. If you use Power Bait, there is a good way to improve its performance for trolling. Take a cotton ball and carefully separate the fibers and spread the ball into a flat disk. Make a pancake of Power Bait of your favorite color, preferably with sparkle, and press it onto the cotton. The two disks should be roughly equal in size. Pick up the combined disks or pancakes, now pressed into one, and knead the mass vigorously to mix the cotton fiber into the dough. Roll it out into a cylinder roughly the diameter of a pencil. Cut into eighth-inch lengths with a sharp scissors and store the resulting nuggets in a Power Bait bottle or other air-tight container. These baits will stay on your hook when trolling much better than the original product.

In salmon eggs, I like the Mike's Shrimp scented salmon eggs. I have on occasion had good results with them.

SCENTS

Corn that is scented as described on page 65 has shown itself to be considerably more effective as kokanee bait than unscented corn. I would venture to say it is the most effective bait I have used on kokes, though this, like the very need for bait, is hard to prove.

There is a company in Oregon called Pro-Cure that manufactures very high-quality fish attractor scents. They make several scents that are quite effective on kokanee and other species. These are high-quality natural scents.

Four good scent combinations—there are many more—are made by mixing equal parts of Sand or Freshwater Shrimp, Shrimp/Prawn, Squid, or Herring Scent and Anise Plus scent into 2 to 3 ounces of corn. All of these scent combinations are effective; you may find some to be more or less effective than others on your favorite lake. The preference of the kokanee for different scents also changes as their mood changes. They often prefer one scent combo one day and another the next.

It is a good idea to treat a new batch of corn every month. It deteriorates if left over a long period of time. Keeping it cool in refrigerator or cooler at all times will maximize its longevity.

To make scented corn, open and completely drain an eleven-ounce can of white Shoepeg. If you feel you need less than the whole can, keep the juice, put the unused corn in it, place it in a sealable container, and freeze it until you make another batch. Use a magic marker to label four low, wide resealable plastic containers and their lids, "Shrimp/AP," "Herring/AP," "Squid/AP" and "Shrimp-Prawn/AP." Place 1/4 of the drained corn to be used into each of the four resealable containers.

Add about fifteen drops or half a teaspoon of Pro-Cure Sand Shrimp or Freshwater Shrimp scent (the two are the same) to the container labeled "Shrimp/AP." Add an equal amount each of the other scents (not Anise Plus) to their respective containers. Next add fifteen drops of Anise Plus Scent to each of the four containers. Stir each thoroughly to get the scents mixed with the corn and with each other. Be careful not to contaminate one container with scent from another. Seal the containers of scented corn and refrigerate, or, if you are ready to go fishing, place them in the cooler.

I like to keep my corn in the cooler until I use it unless the weather is cool. I carry a separate small cooler on the boat for corn, maggots, and plastic lures like Vance's Bugs.

Other scent combinations you may want to try include Herring/Sardine, Shrimp/Squid, and Squid/Herring, all with Anise Plus. Once you learn what the silvers in your area like, you may want to mix only 2 or 3 portions of scented corn for a trip. Some scent combinations seem to be more effective in some areas, others in others. Of course, the kokes may prefer one scent combo one hour, and another the next, so it pays to have a few from which to choose.

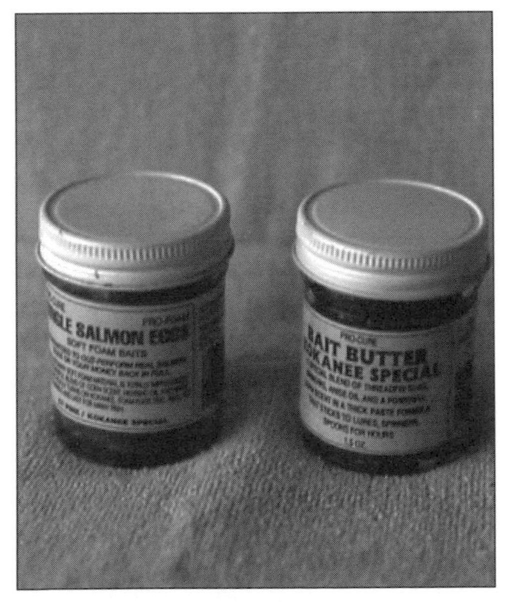

Pro-Cure scented foam eggs.

Pro-Cure sells Anise Plus Scent with and without a pink color. With or without may make a difference in the scent's effectiveness. Kokes may go "clear" one day and "pink" the next.

As to the problem of fishing where corn is illegal, Pro-Cure sells little "eggs" made of plastic foam. You can buy them scented and colored in a bottle like salmon eggs, or you can buy them dry and apply the scent yourself. They come in a variety of scents, each with its distinct color, including Salmon Egg (red), Shrimp (pink), Predator/Anise/Fish Oil ("optic pink"), Cheese (glo orange), Shrimp (chartreuse), Corn (white), and Kokanee Special (hot pink). I like to treat the foam eggs as outlined above for scented corn, adding an equal volume of corn scent to each container. The foam eggs are tough and last a long time. You do need to refresh the scent on your foam eggs periodically. I like to change foam baits frequently, putting used ones back in the container of scent to freshen up.

Not too long ago, I ran out of Pro-Cure foam eggs, and was ready to go fishing in Utah. I cut some clean foam ear plugs up into small chunks and soaked them in my various scent combinations. They seemed to work just fine.

Another good bait for areas where corn is illegal is shrimp. Purchase half a dozen fresh shrimp tails with the exoskeleton still on. Clean and shell them and split each in half along the "vein," which is really the gut. Cut each C-shaped piece in half. Now you have several slightly curved pieces about an inch long, depending on the size of the original shrimp. Cut these into strips about 1/4 inch in diameter.

Place your shrimp strips into a resealable container and add 15 drops of the scents you deem most appropriate. I have used Herring/Anise Plus, Squid/Anise Plus, Shrimp/Anise Plus, and Herring only. I have caught kokes on all.

I use corn of only one scent combination on each lure at a time. I often put corn of different scents on different lures at the same time, however. If I start getting hits on one scent combo, I switch the other lures to that.

Pro-Cure also makes their scents in "butter" or paste form to go on hard lures, and in what they call "sauce" for soft plastic lures. The trouble with the butter and sauce is that they do not spread scent out into the water well if the water is cold. For cold water, a better choice is to use Pro-Cure adhesive-backed foam scent pads and the liquid scents.

I have had good results with WD-40 as an attractor scent. Many anglers spray WD-40 on lures and bait. Why fish like the smell of this stuff is more than I can say. I do have two hypotheses, however.

One is that it masks human scent. The other is from researcher Charlie White in Canada, and suggests that fish are attracted to amino acids and oil does contain those. In his experiments with various scents, White found used motor oil the most effective scent available.

Tom Capelli, a New Mexico guide who is very successful on kokanee, trout, and mackinaw, uses WD-40 quite often, especially for the macks. He is convinced, after thousands of hours of fishing, that it increases strike frequency.

John Skibsrud, who slays big kokes at night on Montana's Lake Hauser, sometimes sprays his bait with WD-40. Hard to argue with his results.

I even hear from bass tournament anglers that many of the professional anglers on TV may advertise a variety of commercial fishing scents, spraying them all over their lures while on camera. When it comes to really needing to catch a bass that may be worth thousands of dollars in tournament prizes, however, these same guys are hunkered down with their backs to the camera, spraying their lures with WD-40.

FOR A SPECIAL OCCASION

In late summer and fall mature kokanee stage together at the mouths of bays in preparation for the spawn. This can happen, depending on the location and strain of kokanee, from mid-August through November. While they are so congregated, and later, as they move toward the tributaries in which they will attempt to spawn, the fish can often be caught with jigs or spinners, or by slowly trolling a spoon or spinner over their heads.

As the kokes move into the bays, however, they can become exasperating to the angler trying to catch them. They will hit spoons, jigs, spinners, and flies, but with low frequency. You can often pull a lure through a school of hundreds of fish without getting a single strike.

Doug Phillips, owner of Strawberry Bay Marina, put me onto the fact that a size 16 treble hook will often outperform most lures in this situation. Cover it with a tiny, elongated gob of "Pink Glitter" Power Bait just large enough to cover the hook. About 48 inches up the line, attach a very small split shot. Drop this rig in among the staged or upstream-bound kokanee and hold on. It will sink slowly and pre-spawn kokes will hit it with better frequency than they do most lures.

Section 3

ANGLING METHODS AND TECHNIQUES

Six

LOCATING KOKANEE

SPRING

One can ride around in a boat and locate good largemouth, smallmouth, or northern pike habitat just by looking. The factors that render a given area suitable for kokanee are mostly invisible. Instrumentation can help, but it cannot see everything.

Preferring open water, kokes will probably be in one of the broader, deeper parts of a lake. Or they may be in a large cove where plankton, for reasons that often have something to do with wind or lake currents, has gathered.

Kokanee like water temperatures in the neighborhood of 50 to 55 degrees F. They will usually be at a depth in the water where they can suspend in these temperatures, provided there is adequate oxygen and food there. If they must go outside their comfort zone to eat, or to escape danger, they will.

Given the lack of good, visible indicators, one cannot just go out on a new lake and immediately find kokanee. It helps to do some homework before you get into the boat.

One good source of information is the local game and fish department. Officials there can put you in touch with the fisheries biologist who works the lake with which you wish to become acquainted. If the biologist has been in the area for a while, and especially if he or she happens to be a kokanee angler, you will probably get some very good information.

By talking with anglers, guides, and marina and tackle shop owners around a lake, you can usually get to know the general locations of kokanee hot spots, approximately how deep they are running, and the lures they are hitting.

Simply watching for congregations of trolling boats is often enough to put you into the kokanee. You may see a whole group of boats seeming to swarm around one common area. There may be two or three; there may be 20. This, in a kokanee lake, is as good a sign as one will see. Get in among 'em and use your finder. But be courteous and thoughtful. Take note of how the others are fishing and steer accordingly.

Once you find the general areas on the lake where kokanee are likely to hang out, take some time to explore those areas with a good fish locator. Doing this repeatedly over a period of time, you will get to know the kokanee of that water and will develop a feel for where schools are likely to be under a given set of conditions.

The bottom line is finding the fish themselves with your locator. This is done more quickly once you know the lake and where the kokanee typically hang out, but it still must be done.

As phytoplankton blooms become more common with the warming spring sun, Daphnia and other zooplankton start to reproduce and become abundant. Kokanee get more active and aggressive. At some time in May or June, this usually brings them near the surface. This is a prime time of year to fish for them. Stirred up by spring plankton blooms, a bit on the lean and hungry side, they are on one of the better bites of the year. Suspended near the surface due to temperature, they are accessible.

This is a good time of year to fish with spliced lead-core line or a chain weight to drop your lure down to the typically required fifteen to twenty-five feet.

Those with electric trolling motors may do much better at this time than those trolling with noisy gasoline engines.

SUMMER

As the water near the surface warms, kokanee will be driven deeper and deeper. How deep depends on the lake and on the conditions surrounding it. In a high elevation lake, or one that lies far to the north, the water will probably not warm too much and the fish will typically go no deeper than 35 feet, in some lakes much less. In a lake that warms readily, they may be at 80 or 90 feet by late August or early September.

Lead-core line can get you down to about 50 feet, if you add chain weights where the lead-core line meets the mono. A one-ounce chain weight and five colors trolled at about 1.2 MPH will get you to about 50 feet, depending on several other variables. Much beyond that, the kokanee belong to the downrigger angler and a few persistent jig fishers.

A good powerful finder is more important now than ever. You need it to reach down there and to show you accurately how deep the kokanee are suspended. Once you know that, and once you have a way to drag a good lure of the proper color by them or just above them, they will hit it as readily as they would in May. Also, they are bigger and stronger than they were in the spring.

LATE SUMMER AND FALL

The Bottom Line Tournament Master SF3 is alarming its fool head off. It is telling me it is seeing more fish than even it can believe. I go to it and turn off the alarm. Indeed the screen shows a huge number of fish stacked at between 35 and 50 feet. Kokanee, getting together and getting ready to spawn. The spawn, a mid- to late fall happening in this lake, will not start for weeks, but already in the third week of September the fish are feeling the drive to congregate at the mouths of canyons.

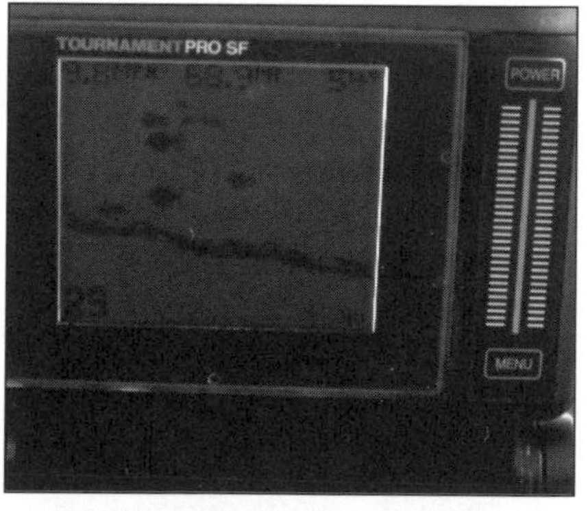

A good finder is one of the kokanee chaser's most valuable tools.

I man the trolling motor and watch the finder in an effort to stay over the kokanee. The three other people on the boat rig up with their favorite jigging combo. One has a small Zzinger that glows in the dark. The hook, suspended below the jig

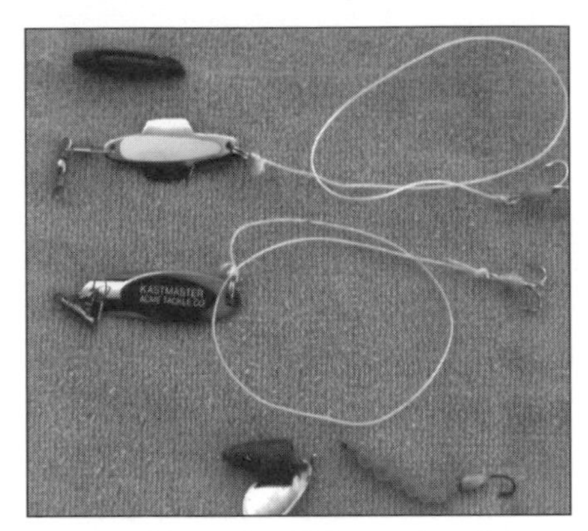

Kokanee jigging rigs. These work well day or night.

Zzingers and Buzz Bombs (which look like minnows) work well whenever jigging is practical.

by a swivel and five-inch leader, is baited with corn. Another goes with a sizable rubber-lined sinker a foot up-line from a Mack's glow hook baited with corn. A third ties on a Kastmaster and threads a single bright blue-green Eurolarva on the Mack's glow hook suspended from it by an eight-inch leader. They estimate the depth of their offerings by counting pulls. Soon they start catching fish.

These kokes are in their prime. They are strong and hard, full of energy, and as large as they will ever be. Some show a definite though subtle pink tint on their silver, blue, and white bodies. One could hardly imagine more beautiful fish.

Finding kokanee in late summer and fall when they are staging in preparation for the spawn is usually pretty easy, if you know a little about the lake and about the habits of the kokanee therein. Start patrolling the mouths of bays and canyons, watching the fish finder. Learn which bays and tributaries are favored by the kokanee. Watch for salmon "porpoising," jumping along the top of the water much like the mammal for which this peculiar behavior is named. You may find them schooled so tightly and in such large numbers that you will believe your fish finder has hiccuped.

Some folks pull the old walleye angler's trick of tying a balloon to the base of the tail (caudal peduncle) of the first fish caught by a length of light line. Be sure it is plenty long enough to allow the koke to go back to his original depth. He will, if released in good condition, return to the school and stay with it, keeping you apprised of its whereabouts.

Handle the kokanee carefully, or he will be so sick when you let him go that he will simply float on the surface and die. This makes sea gulls happy, where they occur. It is surprising what a large fish a little gull can swallow.

As the spawn begins, the kokanee will be distributed from the main lake near the mouths of bays well up into the creeks and canyons where they spawn. The farther you go up the canyon or tributary, the higher the percentage of red fish you will encounter.

The fish remaining out in the reservoir or lake will still provide good fishing. Those farther up in the bay will be more reluctant to bite.

In many lakes there are more than one strain of kokanee. They may spawn at different times. The early spawn usually runs up any suitable tributaries that are available. It usually starts in early fall—perhaps as early as mid-August—ending by November.

The late spawn normally takes place in the lake proper. Kokanee stack in the lake off some suitable gravel bar or shale bank, spawning there later. In Flaming Gorge, early spawners run up Sheep Creek in August through October. Starting in late October or November, the late spawners make their redds in some exposed and crumbling shale outcrops on the west side of the lake.

The Gorge also has a late run up Green River. About 90 percent of the fish in the Gorge are late spawners. This provides the fisher with two opportunities each year to take stacking kokes. Check regulations; some states prohibit the keeping of red kokanee. Others have definite rules concerning snagging or foul hooking and how far up the tributary you can fish.

Many lakes have no suitable spawning sites. Kokanee gather in bays or along bars or banks or at dams, but it is all in vain; there is nowhere suitable for them to lay their eggs. They still stack early at the mouths of bays and canyons, however, and can still be caught there.

Steve Emrick and Rob Clifford

Home-made ice-fishing sled and bucket can carry all the equipment necessary for ice fishing.

WINTER

Kokanee are caught through the ice in many areas. As at other times of the year, the best source of information in winter is probably the knowledge of other anglers or the local state biologist or game warden. On some lakes there seems to be no one good place, the kokes being intermixed with trout and other species. In other lakes, kokes can occasionally be singled out and caught in great numbers, as they often are in Porcupine, near Logan, Utah and Georgetown, near Anaconda, Montana.

A good portable finder like the Bottom Line Fishing Buddy II or the Vexilar FL-8 flasher is no less an advantage for ice fishing than in the summer. One can tune in on fish activities and more quickly learn where to catch the little bounders.

Some lakes do not ice over in the winter. Kokanee can be taken in these from a boat by trolling very slowly with the same equipment used in summer.

It is a curious thing having to do no doubt with the temperature dynamics of individual lakes, but kokanee can be found shallow during the winter and early spring in some lakes and may be 80 feet deep in others. Tons of kokanee were taken near the surface in Roosevelt Reservoir in Washington during the late winter of 1995-1996. At the same time, the kokanee in Navajo Reservoir in New Mexico were hovering at 80 feet and were not overly cooperative.

TROLLING TECHNIQUES

Seven

GETTING STARTED

Probably 80 percent of the kokanee caught across the country are caught by trolling. Trolling is fun and productive. In seven days of fishing on Lake Paulina in Oregon, Phil Johnson and another angler took 105 kokanee. Their method? Trolling, exclusively.

Many other good anglers consistently limit out also. There are guides like Tom Capelli of New Mexico, Joe Hackett of New York, Randy Wiig of Colorado, and Vance Staplin of California who take folks out for kokanee; if they get skunked, they face a boatload of unhappy customers. What do these guys do to increase their chances of success?

The first step, as outlined in Chapter 6, is finding the kokanee. Don't worry too much about water temperature or what the plankton is doing. Use your finder and look for the fishes. Who cares whether they are hot or cold or what they are eating? Seeing them on the finder is the best indication of where your lure should be running.

Once you locate the kokes, you want to troll so as to drag your lures a few feet above the fish. Kokanee see up better than they see down.

I cannot overemphasize here the importance of good electronics. You could do better with a hand line, a can of corn, and a good fish finder than with a $500 rod and reel, a big tackle box full of the finest lures, and no locator. Those schools of kokanee have a lot of empty water around them; you will catch many more fish when you get your lure close to them.

Not only is it prudent to have the best electronics you can afford, it is also necessary to know how to use this valuable equipment. A good idea when you purchase a finder, or if you are not very familiar with yours, is to spend several hours out on the lake going through the instruction book, getting to know your finder, to know its automatic and manual modes and how to best take advantage of them to get the most information you can about "down there."

Understand that how a fish is oriented may have more to do with the size your finder shows it to be than how large it really is. If it is oriented parallel to the boat, it may be hit with more pings (the pulses of sound sent out by the transducer) than if its orientation is perpendicular to that of the boat. It will therefore show up larger on your screen than it would otherwise.

Learn about the range setting; if kokes are suspended down no farther than, say, 40 feet, what is the use of leaving the range on auto and scanning all the way to the bottom, which may be 300 feet away? You will only lose resolution scanning water in which you really are not interested. Better to manually set your range to 60 feet.

A good downrigger like the Cannon Easi-Troll II is the best way to get a lure to a known depth.

Finders have gotten much easier to use in the last few years, but getting the most out of them still takes a little practice. And as you practice with your finder, you will learn surprising things about the lake you are on. It would be difficult to spend your time more productively.

USING DOWNRIGGERS

Downriggers are installed on boats in a variety of ways. If you plan to install some on your boat, get help from your dealer, service personnel, or a knowledgeable friend. How they are installed will have much to do with the fun you have with them in the years to come.

On a small, tiller operated rig, two downriggers are typically enough. A pontoon or large fishing rig can handle four or more, but you quickly reach a point of diminishing returns. I would rather have fewer downriggers and spend the extra money in better electronics. I seldom run more than three downriggers, even from a wide pontoon boat.

Downriggers can keep you busy on a fishing trip, but they are not difficult to master. Most have a rod holder as part of the downrigger. To set one up, put the rod in the holder and leave the drag on the reel very loose. Attach the ball to the end of the cable and make sure the clip is closed securely. Now attach the clip of a downrigger release of your choice to the top eye on the back of the ball, or to a stacker that you have installed on the cable above the ball.

Most downrigger releases work somewhat like the old-time clothes pins, the back end of which were squeezed to open the front. But there are many different systems. Be sure you understand how your releases work before you go fishing.

Clamp the release onto your line with a fairly light setting. Kokanee are not all

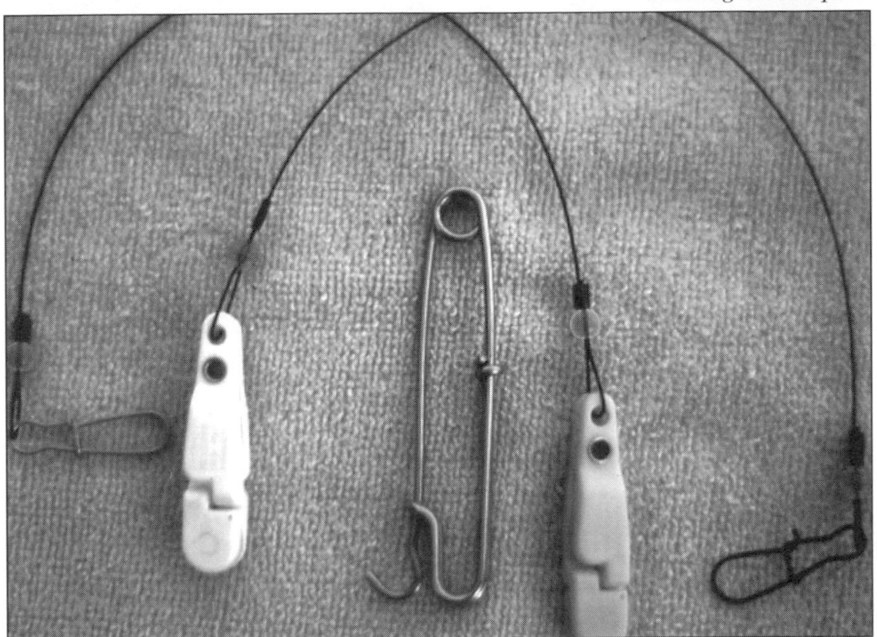

Off Shore downrigger releases, sold by Sep's and Vance's, are simple to use and just right for kokanee.

that large and cannot pull the line free of the release if it is set too tightly. You will get a feel for this with your release, but only after considerable trial and error. If the setting is too light, the line will come free when you do not want it to. If too heavy, the line won't pop out of the release when a fish hits your lure.

If your downrigger is manual, slowly and carefully loosen the clutch and allow the ball to go gently into the water. If it is electric, set it to descend slowly. Everything needs to be done gently, in order not to pull the line free of the downrigger release. When the ball or stacker is at the surface of the water, set the depth counter to "000."

Some folks disengage the line on their reels when dropping the downrigger ball, as one would when casting. I prefer to simply loosen the drag until the line flows with very little resistance. Watch the rod and reel as the ball drops, making sure that the line is flowing off the reel smoothly. Here is where a good quality drag comes in handy.

Slowly drop the ball until it reaches the desired setting. It will work best if the boat is moving slowly as you do this. If your finder tells you that kokes are suspended around 30 feet, you may want to run the ball at 22 to 26 feet.

When the ball is at the depth you desire, tighten the clutch. Tighten the drag on your reel and bring in line until there is a considerable bend in the rod.

When the kokanee are 30 feet or more down and the water is not too clear, it is seldom necessary to run your dodger more than 6 to 8 feet behind the ball. Kokanee are usually less jumpy than trout, and usually don't give a hoot about the downrigger ball. But like all rules one attempts to apply to animals, this one applies sometimes, sometimes not. The salmon will be frightened by the downrigger ball occasionally.

If you feel they are shying from the ball and you are running a big lake troll attached to the ball, remove it. With clear visibility, the troll may be a bit too much for the fish.

If removing the troll does not help, try dropping the dodger and lure back 20 or 30 feet from the ball. You may have to increase that distance to as much as 100 feet.

Another trick worth trying is to run the ball 15 or 20 feet below the kokanee, attaching your release to the cable with a stacker. Say, for example, the kokes are suspended between 18 and 25 feet. Run your ball down to 20 feet, attach the stacker and release to the cable, then run the ball down another 15 to 18 feet. The dodger and lure will be running off the cable right above the kokes and the ball will be traveling out of sight and mind at 35 to 38 feet. Just be sure you know where the bottom is.

It may be helpful to camouflage the ball, or to turn it into an attracting device. Some feel a red ball spooks fewer fish than black. I use a black, 10-pound ball much of the time. I have covered the sides of the ball with Real Image tape with holograms of fish on it. I don't know if it helps. I catch fish, but I may without the tape.

Ball size may be a factor. Who knows how much a fish can tell about the mass and size of that ball just by the vibrations it emits? If you are trolling shallow, you don't need much weight to hold your cable straight. I use a 10-pound ball at 40 feet or more. At less than that, an 8-pound ball does fine. A 6 is good at 20 feet or less, and may be less spooky.

GETTING THEIR ATTENTION

Imitate a School of Baitfish

Large trolls are very effective as attractors of fish. They seem to mimic the flash and vibration of a fleeing school of baitfish. This as much as anything in the world will trigger a strike from most any large fish that commonly chases smaller fish.

It is not uncommon to see large trolls used as in-line tackle. The setup usually is lead-core, steel, or mono line, perhaps a lead weight, a big lake troll, a snubber, then a leader from 2 to 10 feet long with a lure at the end of it.

There is no denying the effectiveness of such an outfit. They catch tons of kokanee, kings, and various species of trout each year. But all that weight on the line demands that the rod and reel be heavy. Together, the heavy terminal rig and heavy rod deaden the action of the fighting fish considerably.

If you want to feel the fight of your fish, the large troll can be hooked to the downrigger ball. You can even hook two or three of them in tandem, using blades of different colors and finishes. This attracts fish just as well as having the troll in line.

Once this is done, there are two common ways of getting a lure into this system where a fish is likely to grab it. First, you can attach a downrigger release to the end of your troll and attach your line to that. The shortcoming of this method is that you cannot put much tension on your rod because it lifts the troll up and out of its normal horizontal line of travel. You then lose the action of the troll and its attractiveness to the fish.

If you run with little tension from the rod, you will have more slack in the line than usual when a striking koke takes the line out of the clip. Even with this flaw,

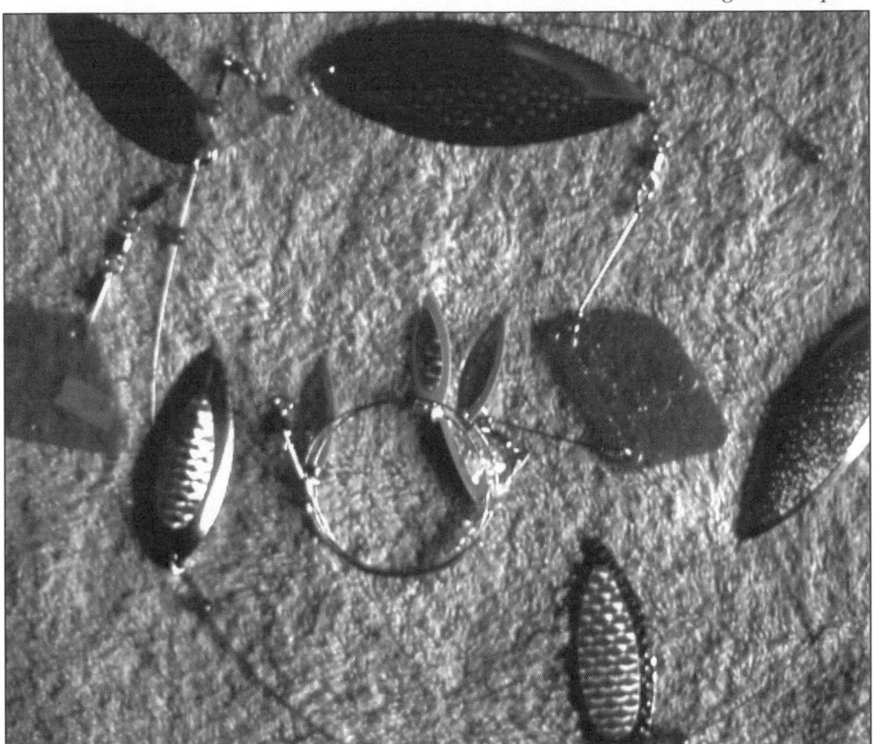

Lake trolls imitate baitfish, attracting the attention of aggressive kokanee.

this is a viable method. I have used it often and prefer it in many ways to the method described below. It just looks, well, sloppy. Folks who see you fishing this way may accuse you of being an amateur.

Some feel you need tension on the rod to hook the fish. Others advocate setting the hook after the strike. I believe the kokanee, with its soft mouth, sets the hook the minute it hits the lure. I do not worry about hooks being set; I worry instead about tearing them loose.

Try running a 0000 dodger or reasonable facsimile on the line about five feet behind the big troll. The dodger seems to increase the strike rate significantly, even with all those blades turning up ahead. I believe the troll calls them in, the dodger focuses their attention on the small lure a foot or two behind it. A dodger will also add action to a lure such as a trolling fly or bug that lacks action of its own.

The other, more politically correct method of using big trolls with the downrigger, is to attach the string of trolls to the ball, then attach a stacker two or three feet above the ball on the downrigger cable. Hook the clip on the release into the stacker and run the fishing line through the release. Rig this outfit so that the dodger and lure travels two to five feet farther back than the end of the string of lake trolls.

Now you can put proper tension on the rod, cranking in line until you get that deep bend you like to see in a rod when fishing with a downrigger. Everything works hunky dory, unless you allow the line to drop low enough to get tangled with the lake troll. Or unless the action of dodger and lure cause line and troll to get together. If that happens, some nightmarish tangles can result. It is best, I think, just to cut them out and re-rig. Less time is lost and nerves are less frayed than if you try to untangle everything.

Make sure you have a container for discarded monofilament. Dropping balls of this stuff into the lake is unconscionable when you consider what it can do to wildlife. A three-pound coffee can or large margarine container with an "X" cut into the plastic lid works very well. Stuff it with mono and you never have to remove the lid until you clean it out and dispose of the contents properly at a trash receptacle.

Attaching the release to a stacker above the trolls has the advantage of putting the lure above the trolls where, maybe, it is more readily noticed by a fish coming in to inspect the troll. This seems reasonable, but I don't know that you get any more strikes with one system than with the other. The force that determines which you use will probably be personal preference.

Keep It Simple

If fish are hitting your lure, you will derive more pleasure from catching them on the simplest rig that works. If I can reach the fish without the downrigger, I prefer not to use it, opting instead for a small chain or banana weight, or 5 or 10 yards of lead-core line spliced into my mono.

One usually needs the downrigger, as kokanee are usually more than 15 or 20 feet down. About the only time the downrigger is not the best way to go is in spring, in winter where kokes stay near the surface, or in cold lakes where they never go deep.

If I need the downrigger, I would rather fish without a dodger or lake troll, using only a lure. And I prefer just a dodger and lure over having to use a lake troll.

One good approach is to start the day with only a lure 6 to 10 feet behind the downrigger ball (assuming fish are more than 20 feet down). If you don't get strikes, add a dodger about 1 to 3 feet in front of the lure, dropping everything back so the dodger runs 6 to 10 feet behind the ball.

Dodger to lure distance depends on lure type; a useful rule of thumb would be one foot for flies, two feet for wedding ring and other spinners and small spoons, three feet for Apex and other plugs or very active lures. It is good to increase these distances slightly in very clear water and to reduce them where turbidity is high. For instance, in very clear water. I may run a Needle fish three feet behind my dodger; in turbid water it may be as close as 18 inches.

If no kokanee are after your lure by this time, you may want to try one of the methods discussed for attaching one or more big lake trolls to your downrigger ball. I feel these methods are only to be used when necessary, after having tried many lures, scents, baits, and color combinations. There are times, however, when these methods are the only ones that catch fish.

Using Light Trolls

Small lake trolls are made to run in line in place of dodgers, Lake Clear Wabblers, etc. Many of these are extremely light and offer little resistance.

My problem with these little trolls is that I have it imbedded in my brain that dodgers are more effective. I do not know that my feelings about this are related

Small trolls like these work well when used on the line ahead of the lure.

in any way to reality. But I do tend to use dodgers by preference. I think the dodgers are definitely better with trolling flies and other lures that need action imparted to them. The back and forth action of the dodger almost certainly renders these lures more effective.

But with spinners, small spoons, crankbaits? Definitely more room for experimentation here. Small trolls have their place, I'm sure. Give them a try. I intend to keep working with them, to explore their potential further.

The Best Attention-Getters

I typically use the small size 0000 dodgers, or I may use a large spoon or Wabbler as an attractor. The spoons being sold by Real Images make excellent dodgers. I have had very good results with the large and medium Real Images Spoon with silver fish scale pattern tape on the sides.

It sometimes works well to put two dodgers in tandem. They should either be the same size, or the one in the rear should be slightly smaller. They can be hooked together

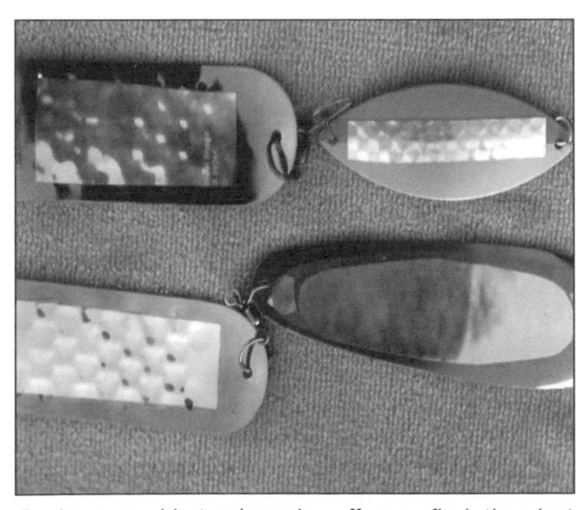

Dodgers used in tandem give off more flash than just one dodger alone. The front dodger, which should be slightly larger and heavier than the rear one, produces little vibration.

with a split ring, with a Duo Lock snap, or with two Duo Locks and a swivel. The swivel gives them a little more freedom to move around and work.

If you use a snubber, use the smallest one you can find. A section of shock gum from Feather Craft is probably best, as it is light and does not deaden lure action. Count its length as part of the distance from dodger to lure. Attach the snubber to the dodger, the leader to it.

Lake Clear Wabbler Blues

Remember the Lake Clear Wabbler? I talked a bit about this animal used as an attractor—like a dodger—in Chapter 3.

When I received my first order of these, I could not wait to get them in the water. So at the first opportunity, I headed for the lake with a fistful of Wabblers.

Just for fun I tied a K-Fly to one of these things. The K-Fly objected, saying that it had no desire to work with this Easterner, but I paid no attention to its protesting. The K-Fly was orange, and the Wabbler I used was chartreuse/nickel and 3.25 inches long. The fly, riding about 14 inches behind the Wabbler, was baited with plain white corn.

I began trolling slowly with the rig alongside the boat, and was pleased with the lazy, wobbly (wabbly) fluttering action and the flash.

I dropped the rig to 27 feet with the downrigger, as I could see several fish around 30 feet on the LCD. It was riding about eight feet behind my big 10-pound downrigger ball, wabbling along at about 0.9 miles per hour. I was planning to rig a second rod, but soon had to stop and reel in this pesky kokanee that would not let go of the fly.

After putting that persistent 16-incher into the cooler, I again proceeded to troll slowly while rigging another rod with another Wabbler, behind which I planned to attach a size 1 and size 0 rainbow colored Needlefish in tandem. I also had attached a narrow strip of Mack's silver fish scale pattern reflector tape to each side of the Wabbler. The Needlefish were hooked together with a duo lock clip. Wabbler to lure distance was to be roughly 20 inches.

Before I even got half way through rigging the second Wabbler, I had to stop and reel in another kokanee. I put it in the cooler, put two more grains of corn on the K-Fly, and sent it back down to the 27-foot depth. And had to stop again to reel in another kokanee, this a healthy 18-incher. "Listen you guys," I declared aloud to the fish, standing alone in my boat in the middle of a 12,000-acre lake, "ya gotta quit botherin' me so I can finish my work. I am trying to learn whether or not these New York lures will work out here, but you all won't leave me alone long enough. If you keep this up, I may have to stop fishing to learn anything."

TROLLING SPEED

Among the successful kokanee anglers I know, most troll at speeds between 0.8 and 1.5 mph. Phil Johnson usually stays between 0.9 and 1.4 mph. Ron Raiha, an outstanding angler from Sandpoint, Idaho, trolls between 0.8 and 1.0 MPH. I troll at similar speeds 98 percent of the time. Occasionally, if nothing else works, I have picked up the catch rate by speeding up to as much as 2.5 MPH, but one has to be careful what lures and attractors he or she is towing, as some act really funny at faster speeds.

The author's daughter-in-law Debra Biser holds a good koke that fell for a Jim Diamond. Note the woolen gloves used to handle the slippery koke.

Dodgers, Wabblers, and many light spoons may start spinning at higher speeds; they may also cease to work if trolled too slowly. You do not want to lose that enticing back and forth motion. Some crankbaits may act in any one of a number of odd ways, others do not mind higher speeds.

Lake trolls and spinners are more speed tolerant. If you decide to go faster or slower than normal, check your attractors and terminal tackle and change, if necessary, to equipment more well suited to the faster or slower trolling speed.

To learn how your equipment acts at different trolling speeds, pull your attractor and lure in the water beside the boat where you can see it and vary your speed until you know at what speeds they will and will not work properly.

As for the fish, they can swim much faster than these speeds, but they may not choose to waste the energy to chase something that swims past too quickly. I believe that is why the slower speeds generally work better for them.

TRIAL AND ERROR

If fish are not striking, there are other ideas to try before varying trolling speed outside the 0.8 to 1.5 MPH range. Take a look at bait, scents, lure and attractor color, lure design, lure size.

If you use scented corn or other scented bait, try changing scents. If you have two types of bait, such as popper maggots and corn, change those. Corn scented with one scent or another will usually outperform other baits. I would exhaust all the different scent combinations with corn before going to other baits.

Be quick and ready to change the color of your lures or the type. I have found that changing from an orange to a chartreuse spinner blade, K-Fly, Vance's Bug, or Apex may change my strike rate radically. Similarly, changing from a spinner to a fluttering spoon or a plug like the Apex or Kwikfish (or vice versa) may do the trick. Often they will shun some of these and practically climb into the boat after one of the others. Even the adding or taking away of a little strip of reflector tape can make a difference.

Quite often, chartreuse lures work well for me in the early morning and late evening, while bright reds and oranges do better in the middle of the day. Fluorescent colors are killers in water that is not super clear, as are phosphorescent finishes.

If changing lure color and type doesn't work, try changing other items. Change from a red to a green dodger, or from hammered nickel to brass, or to one with a hologram of a fish on the side. If you have a small troll on your line, swap to a dodger or to a Flash Lite, or vice versa. Try strips or patches of reflective tape of different colors on your dodgers, lake troll blades, or lures.

It is a good idea to have more rods aboard than you can legally or practically troll at one time. Then if the fish get picky, you can be rigging one rod with a new lure, attractor, or bait while another is in service. Sooner or later, something will work (or the mood of the fish will change and you will think something worked) and you will start catching kokanee.

Watch other boaters and see if anyone is catching kokanee. If they are, try to determine what they are doing and mimic that. A good pair of binoculars is helpful here. I recommend a good-quality, waterproof model like the Burris Signatures in 8X42 or 10X50.

THE CASE FOR SUBTLETY

If kokanee are suspended at 30 feet or less, or if you think they are being spooked by the downrigger ball—or if you tire of the downrigger as I do occasionally and yearn for a simpler method—consider spliced lead-core line. This is a wonderful and carefree way to troll, once you get the depth figured out. It consists of tying in a known length of lead-core line with mono backing and a section of mono between the lead core and the lure.

A good rule of thumb to remember is if fish are 20 feet or less from the surface, splice in one ten-yard section. If they are 20 to 30 feet deep, splice in two. If 30 to 40 feet, three. You can then fine tune your depth by letting more or less backing off the reel. You can also go with a half or a quarter of a color, if the kokanee are really near the surface. If you are nearly down far enough, but not quite, consider adding a small chain weight or split shot above the dodger.

I seldom go to three sections. That is 90 feet of lead-core line and is heavy. If the kokes are over 30 feet, I go to the downrigger. I often use the downrigger if they are over 25, since I like the feel of a rig with one section of lead core, but I like it a lot less with two. But that is personal preference; anything up to three sections and 40 feet is feasible.

I use 20 to 30 feet of 8-pound green mono leader after the lead core, and tie into 10- to 14-pound mono backing on my Garcia 6500 C3 reel. I keep a reel, rigged and ready to go with one 10-yard section of lead-core line, on a medium-light rod.

If I find kokes spooky, and at 20 feet or less, or even a tad over 20 feet—and if I am in the mood—this rig gets put into service.

You can accurately estimate the depth at which your lure is running with Bead Tackle's Depth-O-Troll II, a process that takes about 15 seconds, so long as you know the length of line out. You can also vary depth by trolling speed, checking with the Depth-O-Troll until you are where your fish finder says you should be.

The great advantage here is subtlety. There are no large sinkers, diver disks, or downrigger balls rushing through the water to spook fish. These factors are always of stronger influence when fish are near the surface. This is a great technique where kokes are spooky and/or where water is very clear.

The advantage of spliced lead core over a whole spool of lead-core line is that there is considerably less weight. The most lead core you use is typically three colored, 30-foot sections. The most I typically use is one. You can still use light gear and you can still feel the fight of that muscular silver devil on the other end of your line.

WHEN THEY SEE YOU TOO CLEARLY

If the water is very clear and the fish are suspended shallow, you may want to try a planer board and draw the lure away from the path of the boat. I occasionally use the planer boards, but only when I feel the necessity.

Planer boards work best when you have a little wind, and it is desirable to troll with the wind as much as possible. Try not to violate the rules of trolling direction in relation to the position of the sun, if the water is clear.

To use a planer, simply put the clip at the rear of the board on the line and pass the line through the small release at the front. You need to preset the pressure of the release to work with your line. Install a rubber-lined sinker three feet ahead of your dodger or lure.

When a fish strikes, the line comes out of the release, which is much like a downrigger release. Then the board simply moves down the line as line is brought in, stopping at the sinker.

To get your lure to a desired depth, use the Depth-O-Troll to get the depth right before attaching the planer board. Then simply attach the planer slightly ahead of where the line enters the water.

You can also swing your lures out of the boat's path and get them down to the proper depth by using a diving disk that has the adjustment on the bottom to force it to travel to the side. This, like the planer board, can keep the fish that see your lure from being spooked by the boat.

TROLLING DIRECTION

Much is said in the books about trolling in an "S" pattern. Doing this covers more water, while allowing the lures on the port and starboard sides of the boat to change speeds and depths, increasing chances of action on both sides of the boat. There are other factors, however, to remember about trolling direction. Some may be more important.

As we discussed in the last section, when using a planer board, it is important to troll more or less with the wind. The boards work much better that way. One can usually troll roughly with the wind without going against the ideas in the next paragraph about trolling and the position of the sun.

In clear water and light wind, the position of the sun has everything to do with the direction you should be headed when trolling. When the sun is high in the sky, trolling direction is not overly important. In the morning or evening, when the sun is low, trolling direction becomes considerably more important.

Wherever the sun is, the important thing is not to troll directly toward it. If it is low in the sky, it is best to troll at right angles to the path of the rays hitting the water. If the sun is low in the East, for instance, your direction of travel while trolling should be roughly north or south. You can troll away from it, although a path perpendicular to the rays is probably better. But if you troll into the low sun, your chances of success will be significantly reduced. The more shallow the fish are suspended, the more important this becomes.

When fish approach a trolled lure, they often come in from the side, fall in behind the lure and follow, then catch up and strike it from behind. Or they may come in all the way from behind. At any rate the likelihood of them hitting the lure from the front is minimal. If you are heading into a low sun, like a cowboy hero riding off at the end of a good, cheap western, the lure is between the fish and the sun and their vision of it is impaired. You are putting the fish in the position you would be in trying to hit a ruffed grouse or a clay pigeon flying between you and a low morning or evening sun.

If you are trolling away from the sun, all the fish behind and to both sides of the lure are getting a good show of its finish and action. They are also in a position to hit it readily. Those behind and to the side nearest the sun will have a good shot if you troll perpendicular to the path of the sun's rays. This way, you won't be wasting the return trip.

If you have reason to go toward the sun, try tacking as sailboats do when needing to head into the wind. Head to port of your destination for a while, then to starboard, then back to port; you will be progressing in the desired direction, and increasing your chances of catching fish on the way.

LURE ACTION

If a fish has too much difficulty catching a lure, it will take a pass or two at it and then desist. Fish work on an "economy of energy" system. If something requires more energy to catch than the fish is likely to gain by eating it, it will break off the chase and go in search of an easier mark. This same rule holds if the fish's motivation is territoriality; if the little guy is too hard to catch and is headed out of your protected area anyway, why waste good energy?

Fish are said to "slap" a lure with their tail. What they are doing, I believe, is making a close pass and bringing that vibration-sensitive lateral line to bear, to feed them information about the lure. If you were to pass an object that was releasing a small noise and you became curious, you might bring an ear near the object in order to better understand the source of the noise. This is very similar to what the fish is doing.

Some lures, Apex is a good example, have ideal action at slow speed, but may be so active when trolled fast that they appear unattainable to the fish. Kokanee, having all they want to eat in the form of slow-moving little water fleas, needn't be as aggressive as, say, coho, browns, or kings that live on small fish.

They are probably less motivated to strike than the predatory species. Perhaps that is why more are caught by those who troll slowly.

Watch your lure at your trolling speed; if its action looks too erratic or too lazy, you may be trolling too fast or too slow for the action of that lure.

Spoons used in tandem include, L. to R., Sep's Secret followed by a Sep's Kokanee Kandy, a small Dick Nite behind a Needlefish, and a Kastmaster leading a Sep's Kokanee Kandy.

Creative Uses of Lures

One neat little rig to try is two Needlefish in tandem. A size 1 followed by a size 0 usually works well. Or try a size 2 followed by a size 1 if your kokanee are large. I like a rainbow-colored size 1 followed by a silver size 0, but I have used many color combinations. The size 1 in chartreuse with red spots makes a bright tail.

Remove the hook and split ring from the size 1 and attach the front split ring of the size 0 to the rear of the size 1 in place of its hook. I normally replace the hook on this rig with a bigger one, or with two in tandem, as the size 0 has a small hook on it. Troll this 20 to 24 inches behind a size 0000 dodger, baiting the hook with scented corn.

An effective alternative is to attach a K-Fly or Vance's Bug to a size 2 Needlefish via a 2- to 10-inch mono leader. Phil Johnson, who showed me both these methods, suggests running the dodger reversed, so that the rear end of the dodger is forward; you get more pronounced side to side action that way. Troll slowly so as not to cause the dodger to roll.

Since learning to use this, I have experimented with several spoons-in-tandem rigs. Here are a few that have worked for me. You can play with the colors.

1. Size 1 Needlefish followed by a small Dick Nite
2. Size 1 or 2 Needlefish followed by a Kokanee Kandy
3. Sep's Secret followed by a Kokanee Kandy
4. Large Dick Nite followed by small Dick Nite
5. Medium Triple Teazer followed by Kokanee Kandy, a size 0 Needlefish, or a small Dick Nite

PLAYING A KOKANEE

What do ya do once the little bounder is hooked and is out there raising hell on the end of your line? You treat it gently, that's what. When it wants line, give it line. Keep your drag loose! Just tight enough to gain line when it is not fighting hard. Work the fish slowly toward the boat, allowing it to go when it insists.

Sometimes it will come in very easily until it sees you or the boat, then it will go berserk. Be ready for this, especially if the fight feels too easy. More kokanee are probably lost right at the boat than anywhere else.

Do not try to rush the issue. If the kokanee puts out that last burst of speed and strength, give in. Let it have line. There is a great tendency in some anglers, when excited, to be in a hurry to get them into the net, particularly once they are near the boat. Fight that tendency. Stay cool, take your time. Give line every time the fish wants it. Eventually it will grow tired and allow you to lead it over the net.

Ron Carrey

Playing a kokanee is an activity that requires patience and care. They cannot be forced, as they are strong and their mouths are very soft.

If it notices the net and makes a break, let it go. You can lead it in again. If you try to force it that last few feet or inches and the fish is fighting hard, chances are you will lose it.

Get a large, long-handled net, preferably in green or black, and use it. Don't try to heave a koke up over the side of the boat as you would a channel cat, bluegill, or small bass.

Jeff Pederson

A nice catch that resulted from good trolling.

TROLLING IS FUN

Trolling is a pleasant activity, and can be extremely productive, partly because of the huge amount of water covered. It is always fun if your attitude is right. Take friends along; that way you have someone to throw in the water if the fishing gets dull or frustrating.

Once you hit a school of fat, muscular, silvery kokanee and have two or three rods with kokes on them at the same time and all turns to pure bedlam, you will be well on your way to becoming a confirmed kokanee addict.

FISHING AT NIGHT

Eight

There are few things I love more than the sounds of the night. Three friends and I sit in a pontoon boat on a 15,000-acre lake in near darkness. There is the weak light of the stars and that of our lights, but the stars, though large, are so far away, and our lights are directed down into the water, and provide only faint lateral and reflected glow. The feeble lights of the marina, a mile away, are visible, but lend no detail to an object in our hands.

Those lights, reflected off the water as they are, remind me of an 1880s Mississippi river boat. I imagine roulette wheels, poker tables, rowdy music, pockets with derringers inside, noisy crowds of men in dark coats and ruffled silk shirts and women in frilly dresses, net stockings, and ankle-high buttoned shoes.

Below us, down in their watery world, little creatures are gathering together in the shine of our boat lights, coming out of the darkness of the lake into an area where their senses tell them there may be opportunity for food. Food is the primary object of their desires, the key word in their prime directive, except in mating season. Following these tiny animals are larger ones, and others larger still, all bent on similar goals.

The "larger still" category is the one in which our interest lies. They too are here for food, greedy little devils.

"Come on over, Chum," puns our oatmeal dispenser to his intended victims, putting his heart into his assigned task of spreading oatmeal chum under the boat. In a sort of New Mexico Cockney, an indescribable, unprintable dialect, he starts singing, though his singing hardly does justice to the original:

> Welcome Monsieur, sit yerself down,
> And meet the best innkeeper in town.
> As for the rest, all of 'em crooks,
> Rookin' the guests and cookin' the books.
> Seldom do you see, honest men like me,
> A gent of pure intent who's content to be,
> Masta of thee 'ouse, dabbling out the charm,
> Ready with a 'andshake and an open palm....1

"One more bloody bar and yer wearin' this salmon in yer ear all night, Gary Morris," explains a critic.

"No one appreciates real talent anymore," grumbles the singer. "Beam me up Scotty, no intelligent life down here."

1. From "Les Miserables" (First Night Records, 44 Seymour Place, London W1H 5WQ). If you have not seen it, do. If you cannot go to see it, buy the soundtrack.

"We appreciate talent, if we see any. Com'on, let's catch some fish."

Wind velocity is nearly zero, so we can hear whatever is happening around us, if we keep our mouths shut, our feet still. A coyote yips, yips again, breaks into a yammering, high-pitched howl. He is joined by others of his kind until the hills around the lake ring with a profusion of yips, yaps, cries, wails, and deep-throated howls.

These guys really put their hearts into their singing. They remind me of the Latinos near whom I lived long ago in Brazil, and later in various parts of our West and Southwest, as they sat together in the evening and sang. Even farther back into my dim past, I can remember my relatives in the Appalachians doing exactly the same, to the tune of mandolin and guitar. Singing for the fun of singing, for the joy of being alive.

Whether from two-legged animals in dank little bars in Sao Paulo or Santos, Latino housing tracts in Arizona or Utah, or the hardwood forested hills and hollows of West Virginia, or from furry critters in the dry New Mexico piñon/juniper forest, it is all the same. It is refreshing, inspiring, exhilarating.

These particular songs make the hair on the back of the neck stand straight. Not from fear, but from excitement. From respect. We are listening to music older and more venerable by far than mankind. Not the original "Ode to Joy," but a version far earlier than ours.

An unidentifiable something splashes in the water nearby. Probably a carp or channel cat. "Alligator!" yells one wise-ass.

Western chorus frogs sing from a backwater somewhere. A great horned owl breaks forth with his deep, "I'm awake, you too."

In the midst of all this symphony there arises another sound. Something like, "Holysmokes,thesucker'stakingmypole!" The volume of the call of this new species drowns out the calls of the other wildlife. There is a scuffling sound, a few expletives, some splashing, then flopping on the floor of the pontoon boat. Several new exclamations escape into the dark desert atmosphere ("Man, this dude is slippery as a congressman!") and then the sound of a cooler lid opening and closing. A flopping, a drumming, the rattle of ice comes from inside the cooler. "Nice koke."

Then, "Ouch! Geeez Gary, you got big feet. Why don't you take them canoes out on the water and walk around?"

"Pay attention to your line, oh Wise One. You're about to lose your rod. You hain't got the sense of an intellectually challenged channel cat."

"Hoooly!" Reel sounds, more scuffling, more flopping and cooler noise, then, "I got your channel cat; cain't say if he was intellectually challenged or not. Bet he's smarter than you, though, not to mention better looking."

A large thump and a clatter of ice—previously contained in someone's cup—being scattered over the ample deck of the boat. "I can't see a thing."

"That's 'cause it's dark, imbecile. You ain't supposed to be able to see anything. You got no feathers on your butt, you don't go whooo-whooo or meow, and you don't have a flashlight. Shuddup and fish."

"So hand me the flashlight; how can I fish when I can't see nothin'?"

"You can't fish in good daylight. Bein' in the dark is probably an advantage for you."

"Yeah? Bet I catch a bigger koke tonight than you."

"All you're gonna catch is a cold, Dummy. You'll be lucky to catch that."

"Afraid to bet, huh? Steak dinner for me and the wife tomorrow night at the Golden Corral? Ya up for it?"

"Sure, easy money. My wife and I could use a good free steak dinner. You're on."

"Good, I'll look forward to seeing you and your checkbook."

All grows quiet again. The coyotes have quit singing and have gone hunting. The owls, frogs, sleepy grebes and ducks, and occasional unidentifiable splashing sounds regain center stage for about10 minutes until, "Got one."

DETECTING BITES

The main challenge to this fishing is knowing when you are getting a bite. The same salmon that slash at a moving lure like a bolt of lightning are exceedingly gentle in mouthing a hook covered with corn and held still. Different folks use different methods to detect the gentle mouthing characteristic of kokanee taking a bait. A few of those methods follow.

One of my favorites is to use Berkley Fire Line in 6-pound test. This line is very fine—about the equivalent of 2-pound mono. More importantly, it has no stretch. By fishing a straight line—no slack whatsoever between bait and rod—I can sit with a loop of the line across my fingers and feel the softest tap. Whenever I feel anything, or think I do, I set the hook. Often there is a kokanee there.

The lake we are on tonight has a plethora of other species, not all as gentle in their approach as kokanee. One must protect his or her rig from going overboard, should the bait be grabbed by a smallmouth bass or channel cat. Some set their rods in holders, leaving the reels so the line will go out if pulled. Others elect to hold the rod with a loop of line across the fingers for sensitivity.

Another alternative is to jig gently with a spinner, spoon, or jig. Buzz Bombs and Zzingers work well for this, as do the Kastmaster, the Swedish Pimple, and Shasta Tackle's Double Dancer. The gentle up and down motion often induces a heavier strike and many fish are simply hooked by accident on the upstroke, though they often take the bait as it falls. The hook is normally suspended from a few inches to a foot below the lure on a short leader. The lure acts as an attractor, getting the fish's attention and drawing it near enough to cause it to notice the bait. If you are allowing the lure and bait to fall and it stops falling momentarily, set the hook.

FISHING LIGHTS

We have lights over either side of the pontoon boat, shining down into the water. Two guys are fishing from each side, and we are catching kokanee and the occasional rainbow. Most nights produce some channel cats; we have one tonight, so far.

The bantering and friendship are as pleasurable as the fishing, which in itself is great. We all work, but it is Friday evening and we are off tomorrow, and are enjoying that brief weekly illusion that we are free humans, owners of our own lives, souls, and destinies. Much of the jocularity is a means of releasing stress built up during a week of doing what we don't really believe in for people we don't really like. Each of us is working on his own plan, his own way of getting out of the corporate life, where they lead you to the water but won't allow you to drink. It is a cool, dark, moonless night in July, very pleasant.

L. to R.: Submersible fishing light, empty Kokanee Beer can, and a floating fishing light. The lights attract kokes at night; the beer does not.

About 20 feet below us, kokanee, cats, and trout continue to gather, drawn by curiosity, by the congregation of invertebrates and small vertebrates that have come to the light, and by the flecks of oatmeal that we stirred into the water and that continue to settle slowly, glittering in the light.

We find oatmeal a very acceptable chum; it reflects the light well and thus shows up. Stirred into the water after soaking a minute or two in the hand, it stays suspended a long time, drawing in critters from the dark water for quite a while before more has to be added. It does not plug up the fish with an indigestible substance as does corn. I owe New York fishing guide Joe Hackett a thank you for this idea.

On the port side of the boat, we have a floating light which is drawing its power from a deep cycle 12-volt battery sitting nearby.

On starboard, we have a bright, handheld lantern lashed to the railing of the boat a couple of feet above the water, shining down. It is an experiment; this is the first time we have tried such a contraption. It seems to be working fairly well. It too is working off a deep cycle battery.

We also have aboard a submersible light with long cables like the others that clip to a 12-volt vehicle or deep cycle battery. Having used it before, we decided to try the lantern. If the surface lanterns had failed to attract enough fish, the submersible would have gone into the water.

All these lights seem to work pretty well. The submersible is by far the most powerful, and brings aquatic critters from farther off, but they seem to suspend deeper when the light is in the water, and we have gotten fish and lines entangled with the light cord, an unpleasant, unnecessarily stressful situation similar to downrigger stress and resulting in similar bad moods and language. Having the light floating right on top of the water on a Styrofoam ring carries most of the same disadvantages, plus the irritating bumping of the light against the pontoon or side of the hull, depending on what boat we are in.

We prefer to have the light suspended a short distance above the water also because we can take advantage of reflected and peripheral light to almost see what we are doing. We don't have to keep another light ready for baiting hooks, unhooking fish, getting soft drinks, though there are flashlights aboard.

Frank Verano, the man called "Mr. Salmon" in Connecticut, uses a Coleman gas lantern, for which he has made a bracket and reflector to direct the light into the water. The bracket clamps to the gunwale of his boat. He is a superb night fisherman, and has taken thousands of kokanee this way.

This process can be done without a large light. Tom Capelli, the kokanee, laker, and trout guide on Heron Lake in New Mexico, has fished at night with Buzz Bombs with a "glo" finish, with no light. He activates the phosphorescent properties of the finish with the strobe flash of a camera, the same way we activate all our phosphorescent lures, day or night.

TERMINAL RIGS

For educational purposes, each of us is using different terminal tackle. One has on a plain single hook suspended eight inches below a small Kastmaster from which the hook has been removed. He is fishing with white Shoepeg corn scented with a mixture of Pro-Cure Anise Plus Scent and Shrimp/Prawn Oil. The second angler has on a red Gamakatsu hook with white glow material on the shank. His hook is suspended about 10 inches below a small Swedish Pimple. He has been changing the colors of his glow hooks periodically. He reactivates the glow properties of the glob of plastic with the camera strobe each time the hook is out of the water. He is baiting his bright hooks with white Shoepeg corn. He alternates the plain corn with the same corn scented with herring or shrimp scent.

The third angler is experimenting with Buzz Bombs and Zzingers in various bright and glow colors. He is baiting with pieces of shrimp that have been scented with sand shrimp oil.

I am using a rig I copied from one sent to me by John Skibsrud of Deer Lodge, Montana. John has forgotten more than I will ever know about night fishing for kokanee. I am baiting with Eurolarvae of various colors and sometimes scented corn.

John's rig resembles a wedding ring spinner without the wedding ring. It features a glow hook, about eight orange beads, a spinner blade and clevis, and a bullet weight that comes down against the beads. All this is on a mono leader about 27 inches long. The bullet weight keeps the line straight and heightens sensitivity.

John says they vary the hook colors and find that kokes will hit one color hook one night and another on another night. They charge the hook's glow properties with a camera strobe. They use maggots and corn for bait, often spraying the bait with WD-40. John and his friends use floating lights, but clamp them to the gunwale to keep them from banging on the side of the boat and getting in the way when kokanee are being netted.

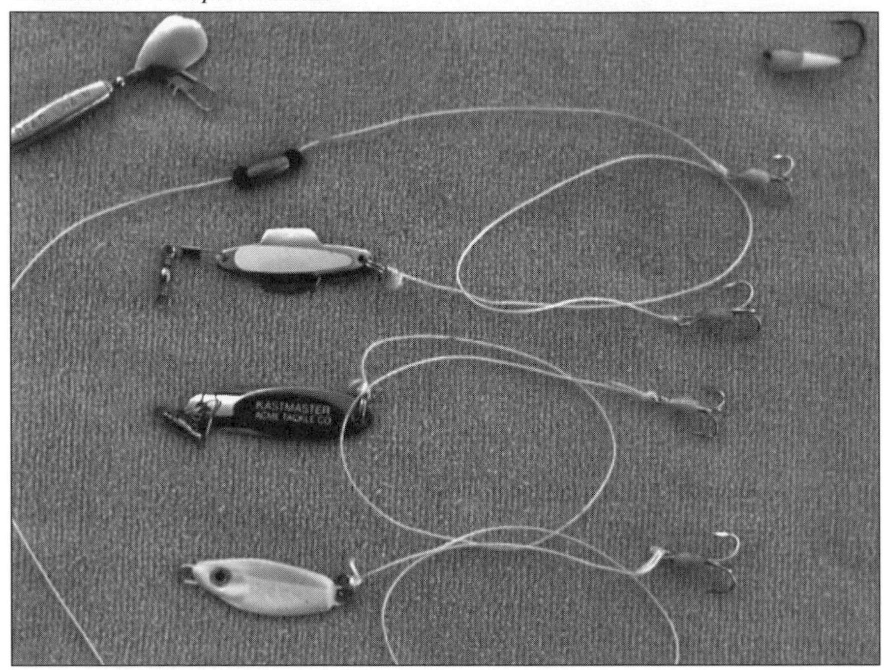

These rigs (thick line has been used in place of mono for the photo) are good for catching kokanee at night. The Jensen Crippled Herring has a glow finish. All the hooks have glow material.

Uncle Larry's Lures of Sacramento, California markets a sort of glow in the dark wedding ring spinner that should be very good for night fishing. It consists of a nickel spinner blade, a row of glow in the dark beads, and a single hook. With a bullet weight and glow hook added, it should be dynamite on dark nights.

Frank Verano uses a baited hook with a heavy sinker just four to five inches up the line. He says the sinker does not scare the kokanee, and needs to be near the hook for him to feel what is going on at the end.

One sometimes catches fish of several species with this process; we have brought in smallmouth, largemouth, and buglemouth bass (carp), channel cats, rainbow trout, brown trout, cutthroat trout, yellow perch, small mackinaw, chubs, and one 10-inch northern pike that looked like a snake with a duck's bill, only it had teeth. Our catch usually runs nearly all kokanee with a few rainbows and browns, an occasional channel cat. It depends on the lake.

HOW FAR DOWN ARE THEY?

A fish locator comes in handy for this. One of the boats we use has a Bottom Line, another has an Eagle, and a third a Humminbird. All work quite well. The most important service they perform in this fishing is not to locate the fish before we start, though that is a valid function of the device, but to tell us the depth at which our customers are congregating on any given night. This can run anywhere from10 to 30 feet or more.

Once we determine the depth of the greatest concentration of fish, we get our terminal tackle to that depth by counting pulls. Some anglers measure the distance from reel to first eye on the rod and pull until their finger touches that, or they may

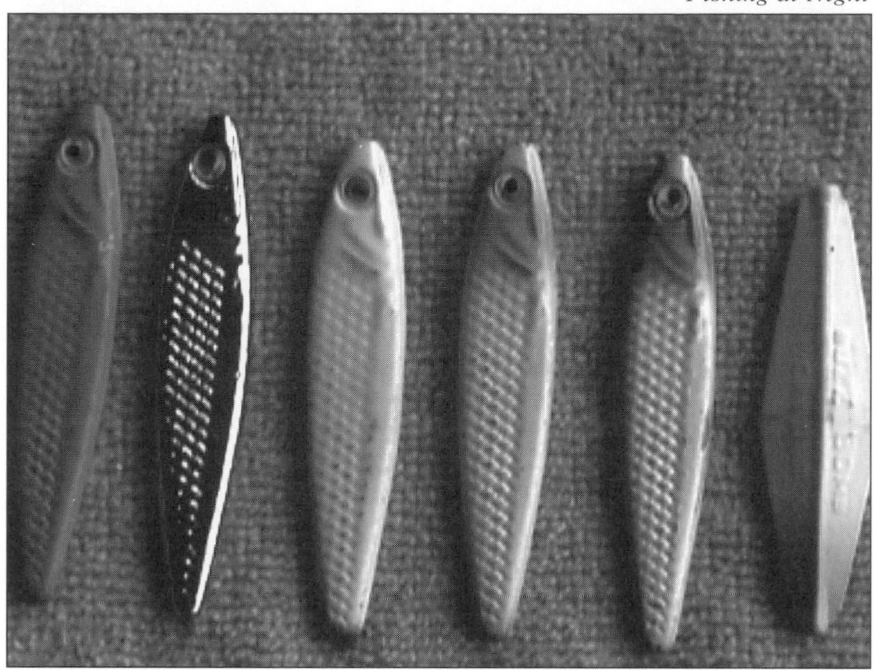

Zzingers and Buzz Bombs work well at night. The third Zzinger from the left glows in the dark.

put a piece of plastic tape around the rod at a predetermined distance. The important thing is to be able to pull a known length of line off your rod and to go from there.

We start counting with our terminal tackle barely in the water and count pulls until the amount of line out roughly equals a tad less than the depth of the fish. Since they see better above them, we try to make things easier for them by putting our baits above them. Considerate, huh? I thought so, too.

There are other methods of measuring the distance. Once Frank Verano finds the depth at which the fish are biting, he cuts a leader that length and then simply drops his line each time until the knot where his line and leader join rests at the surface of the water. Once he is set, no counting is necessary. Frank also uses this method for daytime stillfishing.

John Skibsrud and his buddies drop their terminal tackle to the bottom and then count crank rotations back up to their desired depth. This seems particularly clever to me, as the finder will tell you both the distance to the bottom and to the fish. Then if you know the amount of line your reel brings in per crank, you have it made. The method will not work in very deep lakes however.

There are reels by Riptide, Shimano, Mitchell, Daiwa, and others that count feet of line out. They are expensive, ranging from around $100 up. They are reputed to be accurate, but I have never used one.

THE MOON

We try to fish on dark summer nights. Full moon nights don't seem to produce as well. I feel that this is because the artificial light has more impact, more contrast to the otherwise very dark water, on moonless nights. Overcast nights seem to be good, regardless of the position of the moon.

There are those who feel that the moon has more to say about fishing success than just the amount of available light. John Alden Knight presented a convincing argument on the full effects of the sun and moon on fish in his book *Moon Up Moon Down*. It is an enjoyable book by a kind man and a competent angler. You can order a copy from Solunar Sales Co., Montoursville, PA 17754. Solunar Sales also markets inexpensive solunar tables and calendars each year.

Another chart based on lunar phases and tides comes in a set called, "Fishing the Average Tide." You can order a set for $10.00 from Lou Smitzer, 6108 Madra Ave., San Diego, CA 92120, 619/582-1594.

So, why go out at night to fish for kokanee? Why do I urge you to try this sport when you could be engaging in a plethora of more interesting and constructive activities, like, say, watching some night-time soap opera, replacing the clutch on your brother-in-law's Dodge, or visiting your in-laws?

There are many reasons. The lonely quiet of dark waters, for example. The sounds of night animals, singing their ancient songs. The cool July night air, so much more pleasant than the merciless sun on July afternoons. The pesky mosquitoes that never give up and the fresh breeze that causes them to lose your scent. The moth that is never satisfied until he does a kamikaze flight into your Pepsi. The outrageous and hilarious antics and exclamations of anglers gone mad trying to tie complex knots in invisible line in the dark. A rod dropped overboard by a dozing angler or pulled overboard by a wide-awake channel cat. The snoring of a "quitter" sprawled on the back bench of the pontoon boat. The quitter's howls of indignation when someone slips a live kokanee into his shirt as he sleeps. The uproarious laughter, insults, dirty jokes, clean jokes, tall tales. The unshakable conviction that life is very, very good, in spite of all the despicable greed and brutality in the world.

And, of course, there is the quality of fishing one sometimes encounters. Joe Hackett, the owner of Tahawus Guide Service at Lake Placid, New York, tells me the best he can expect on a good day trolling is around five fish per hour. It is not unusual at night, he says, to bring in 20 fish per hour. ""Most anglers troll on sunny days for kokanee," says Joe, "but fishing at night with a lantern over the boat in the heat of the summer can result in unbelievable action."

John Skibsrud sent me a photo of part of one night's catch on Hauser Lake, up near Helena, Montana. It looked like all his kokanee ran well over a pound with some around three, and there were lots of them.

An angler from the Northwest tells me that some lakes in Washington and Oregon are starting to get crowded at night with kokanee anglers. The word is getting out.

OTHER METHODS

Nine

STILL FISHING

Next to the town of Spirit Lake in northern Idaho is a small lake called, of all things, Spirit Lake. The anglers at Spirit Lake have developed an unusual method for catching their kokanee. Kokanee are caught in the late spring and early summer, before vegetation fills the lake. To get the bait to drop quickly a chain weight spinner by Bead Tackle is attached to the end of the line. A Mack's Glo Hook is attached to that by a 10- to 12-inch leader. The hook is baited with corn or maggots. This whole setup is dropped into the water, lowered to the correct depth for the day, and jigged slowly up and down. When I was there, the catch limit for kokanee was 50 fish per day. Many anglers limit out.

This is a good rig for jigging and baitfishing kokes. I found the chain weights with spinner blades in Spirit Lake Taxidermy, where owners Gary and Diane Berg explained their use to me. If you go to Spirit Lake, be sure and stop in and get to know these friendly people.

I have since used bead chain spinners elsewhere with considerable success. The spinner blade on the chain weight acts as an attractor, as does the glow material on the hook. You know kokanee; like raccoons, they cannot resist anything shiny. Once the koke sees and smells the corn or maggot, he knows what to do with it.

The kokanee at Spirit Lake are tiny. A 10-incher is a wall hanger. Some years ago, the anglers that fish the lake complained to the Idaho Fisheries division about the small size and "slow growth rate" of kokanee in Spirit. Biologists studied the problem and soon learned that the kokanee in Spirit were growing faster than those in nearby Coeur d'Alene Lake. The problem was that 99 percent of the kokanee were being caught as 2+ (two years old) rather than as 3+ and 4+ mature fish.

Spirit Lake is a popular fishing spot, and catch limits on kokanee have been kept high. Idaho Fisheries officials offered to drop the catch limit, a change that should allow more Spirit Lake kokes to reach maturity, but area anglers let it be known that they would prefer to catch lots of little kokanee.

The most popular rig on Georgetown, near Anaconda, Montana, is a single hook or glow hook baited with corn and suspended below a small Swedish Pimple. Like Spirit, Georgetown has so much plant growth that trolling is not practical. Folks who grow proficient at fishing Georgetown take hundreds of kokanee every year. Fishing that lake, which also has some fine fishing for brookies, is not quite as simple as it sounds, as about 5 percent of the anglers take about 95 percent of the kokanee there.

The factor that renders this stillfishing for kokes difficult is the gentleness with which these fish take bait. The average fisher will not notice 90 percent of the bites he or she gets, not knowing how to detect them. A trick used by old-timers on Georgetown consisted of using a small float and watching it carefully. The line from float to weight and on to the bait had to be slack-free. When a koke took the bait, it moved the float oh so slightly, and the angler set the hook.

With the newer, Swedish Pimple (small Kastmasters also work for this) method, the Pimple is put on the line without the hook. A leader about a foot long is attached to the other end of the Pimple. At the end of that leader is a glow hook baited with corn or maggots.

The modern angler often uses a spring bobber as a strike indicator. This is a device about three inches long that attaches to the end of the rod. It has an eye in it, and is made of springy steel. A bead on the end of the device enhances visibility. The rod is set down and propped, as holding it in the hands produces too much motion in the spring bobber.

The line is run through the eye of the spring bobber; the bait/Pimple rig is fished on a tight line as already described. If a koke so much as touches the bait, the tip of the spring bobber is moved, exposing the potential bait thief.

In order to see this action, the rod has to be placed so that the tip can be seen from the side. The motion is slight and vertical; you cannot see it while looking down on your rod tip from behind.

That spring tip is so sensitive that not only can the angler tell when the small Swedish Pimple has settled to the end of the line, he can tell when the glow hook and bait take up all their slack.

It is nothing for an angler who is proficient at this method to take 50 or more fish per day. There is no limit on kokanee at Georgetown.

A technique many of us use while stillfishing during the day or night is to hold a loop of line in the hand. Again, the line from your hand to the hook must be free of slack. When the fish mouths your bait, you will feel it much more clearly than when simply holding the rod. This is a modification of the technique used by certain highly skilled anglers on whitefish, another nibbler. There is more motion to sort out when you are in a boat, given the motion of the boat due to wave action and moving bodies. It can get quite tricky; still, you can develop a feel for it. A light, non-stretch line like 6-pound Fireline works well for this.

Another method for hooking these sneaky fish was described recently in *The Outdoor Press* in an article on Loon Lake by John Merriman of the Tackle Box, a sporting goods store near Loon Lake. I greatly enjoyed John's description of what he calls paranoid fishing; he says, "If you even think a kokanee is looking at your bait, gently but firmly set the hook. If your rod tip stops wiggling in your shaky hand, set the hook. And just for the heck of it, every minute of two, set the hook. You have to become a hair trigger mousetrap and give your complete attention to catching these silvers. Once you get good at this, trout are easy pickin's for you, to say nothing of panfish."

JIGGING

Some of the best jigs for this work are Buzz Bombs and Zzingers in red, pink, orange, pearl, perch or glow finish. Small jigging spoons like the Crippled Herring,

Krocodile, Kastmaster, and Swedish Pimple can also be effective.

I have occasionally had good luck with crappie jigs such as those made by Mister Twister. I like the glow-colored heads by Mack's for this technique. Go for tails in bright colors such as chartreuse, red, orange or pearl. Mack's has a good selection of these too, including a white glo and several fluorescent colors. A drop of Pro-Cure Sand or Freshwater Shrimp scent on the lure seems to help, as does tipping the hook with scented corn.

FISHING PRE-SPAWNERS

A situation in which stillfishing for kokes is productive is when they gather together in large schools prior to spawning. One must keep in mind that the kokanee staged at the mouth of the bay and those already running up in the bay can act quite differently.

Up in the Bay

I am sitting alone in a fine little wooden boat in a bay off Strawberry Reservoir, Utah. It is a lovely August day, not really hot at this altitude, but warm and clear and beginning to look and feel like autumn. On the nearby hills, some of the leaves on the aspens are starting to show a golden tint. Elk will soon be bugling in those aspens; sounds like that, combined with golden and red leaves, the smell of leaf mold, and the crisp, clear air all contribute to making autumn so great.

Under the water, the color red is everywhere as kokanee, nearly ready to spawn, are heading upstream. Many are coming into the bay; a few have already entered the stream at the head of the bay.

They are crazy, these fish. They jump and porpoise beside my boat. There are hundreds of them in the bay, there is one in the air near my boat every 30 seconds or so.

Spawning kokanee are not supposed to take food, but then neither are spawning chinook, coho, Atlantic salmon or steelhead, and all of those are caught as they run up rivers from the ocean to spawn. Why not give it a go?

I once asked Ron Raiha, a man with a remarkable understanding of fish, wildlife, and the ecology of his area, why he thought spawning kokanee, some of which have little digestive system left, still try to eat. "You still look at pretty young women, don't you?" he asked, eyeing my dumpy, middle-aged frame. "The drive is still there even if one can do little about it."

The spot in which I have anchored is well up into the bay. These kokes are much farther along in the spawn than those staged at the bay's mouth. I tie on a Mack's Jeweled Alge and cast it out. It looks good in the clear water, but the kokanee are running about four feet deep, except when they make a run to the surface and porpoise along for 10 feet or so. My lure is running barely under the surface. They show no inclination to rise to it.

I retrieve the lure and install a Bead Tackle chain sinker/spinner about 30 inches ahead of the lure. I cast it out.

The weight carries the lure toward the bottom rapidly; I begin to reel in line. During some of the first several retrieves, a few kokanee follow the lure or flash by it to check it out with their lateral line sensors, but none strike.

These kokanee were taken from the same spot in a bay early in the spawn. They hit a spinner with hammered nickel blades.

On about the twentieth cast, one hits it hard and is hooked. I fight her, a silvery female with no hint of red on her, for a long time before I am able to get her into the net. She runs the drag on the little Zebco 33 Classic several times and, since I have no snubber, I fear the hook will pull out.

Finally I lead her into the net. She is 18 inches of pure silver energy, a beautiful thing as she lies there in my net. For the next three hours, using every lure combination I can think of, though hundreds of kokanee pass under the boat, I get about 10 strikes and land four more fish. In addition to the silver female, I keep one red male. The others, two red males and a red female, I release to go on about their business of making kokanee.

I notice that the fish here in the bay are a mixture of red fish that are ready to spawn and silvery ones that look as if they just came around to see what's going on. They appear to be mature fish, these silvers. I find it surprising that I have gotten more strikes from red fish.

Doug Phillips, owner of the marinas on Strawberry, recently told me of another way to catch the nearly ready to spawn fish. I mentioned it elsewhere in the book, but here it is again. I have had a chance to try it only twice, but it has worked quite well.

Rig with a very small snelled treble hook. Size 16 will do. Place a small split shot about 48 inches above the hook. Bait the hook with a small gob of pink glitter Power Bait just large enough to cover the hook. Doug says he forms his into an elongated form, somewhat like a small worm. When dropped in among the fish, this rig sinks quite slowly, and these kokanee that do not eat hit it with fair

These kokanee were taken later in the spawn in a bay while the author fished with tiny pieces of Pink Sparkle Power Bait on a size 16 treble hook with a very small shot about four feet upline.

consistency. Landing them with this rig takes great care and patience.

Two other lures with which I have had success on these finicky fish are the Thomas Buoyant in fluorescent orange with a rectangular piece of silver scale tape just behind the "gill cover," and a size 2 Rainbow Needle fish. On several occasions, the Needle fish has caught fish for me when no other lure would, though it too is sometimes snubbed.

At the Mouth of the Bay

The fishing is better if one goes out farther into the bay, toward the main body of the lake and finds staged kokanee that are not nearly so ready to spawn as these. Those fish will hit a lure much more readily than the fish farther along in their metamorphosis.

Not too long ago, Vance Staplin of Vance's Bug fame told me he had had excellent results on prespawn kokanee using a plain white 1/4-ounce marabou jig. I have since tried this lure and found it to be quite effective. Two grains of scented corn on the hook enhances productivity.

Jigging or baitfishing over a school of stacked kokanee can provide good action. As with jigging in some of the smaller, weed-choked lakes, I like Buzz Bombs and Zzinger jigs for this work. I also like small jig heads with bright orange or chartreuse Mr. Twister type tails.

One can often catch the congregated fish by simply trolling over them with a big wedding ring spinner, an in-line spinner like the Arnie's or Vibric Rooster Tail, a fluttery spoon like the Needlefish or the Thomas Buoyant, or a lure such as the

Apex or Flatfish. Get their depth, troll low over their heads. Bait the lures with scented corn, scented strips of shrimp, or scented foam eggs.

ICE FISHING

Kokanee are sometimes caught through the ice. This is an extremely popular method at Georgetown Reservoir, where kokanee are so numerous they are considered to be pests by some anglers and biologists. Catches of 50 to 60 fish in a morning of angling are not uncommon. Most are kept and canned or smoked, as there has been no catch limit for kokanee on Georgetown for many years. Most are caught on Glo Hooks baited with corn or maggots. There is a subtle art to this type of angling, and experienced anglers catch many times the fish caught by novices.

The method used here is basically the same as described under "Stillfishing." The difficulty again is the stealth of the fish in taking bait.

Ice fishing for kokanee is also popular at Porcupine Reservoir near Logan, Utah. Some anglers there seem to know where kokes will be at a given time. A popular and effective bait here is the red salmon egg.

Kokes will take ice flies, small jigs, and the Mr. Twister type jigs that all species seem to like. They will also take corn, worms, salmon eggs, maggots and wax worms. Any of these baits will do well on a jig.

William H. Mullins

In Idaho's Payette River, kokanee search for suitable spawning sites.

Kokanee of this size do not grow where the fish are over-populated, and the food supply is limited.

FLY FISHING

Kokanee lend themselves to fly fishing only on rare occasions. They can sometimes be caught with small fluorescent orange or chartreuse wet flies or egg imitations in fall as the spawn is starting to roll. If you know of a fairly narrow bay into which a creek empties that kokanee ascend during the spawn, you may do well on the kokanee in the bay as they begin to move up to spawn. A bright streamer may work well for these pre-spawn fish.

In the fall of 1994, I watched a young man take a five-pound kokanee on a fly in such a bay in Utah. He fought the fish for over 30 minutes. I seriously doubt he will ever forget the experience. He was fishing for cutthroats when the kokanee hit. Fishing for these spawners is generally slow. Though each cast puts your lure or fly in plain sight of many fish, the vast majority of them simply are not in the mood to strike. Most ignore your offering and go their way. On the above mentioned fall day in 1994, several men were fly fishing in that same bay. Kokanee probably outnumbered cuts and rainbows in the bay by at least 20 to one at that time. Though I saw them catch-and-release many cutts, the five-pounder caught on the fly was the only kokanee I saw caught by any of the fly fishers.

Kokanee can also be found in the bays in spring. Occasionally a mayfly or midge hatch occurs in a bay while the water temperature is still low enough to permit kokanee to be near the surface. Nymphs may be traveling to the surface from the bottom of the bay. During this time, kokanee may occasionally be found feeding on the young insects as they ascend to the surface. They may also rise and feed in the surface film itself. When they take insects on the surface, they will often do so in a motion that resembles the porpoising of the fall, but without leaving the water. The angler can see their direction of travel and place a fly that roughly matches the hatch in their path. Unless one spends considerable time on a lake, he or she may never witness this phenomenon, but fishing can be good if the angler is there at the right time with fly equipment.

In the summer on high mountain lakes, kokanee will occasionally feed near the surface when the water is cool in the evening or morning. One can use a fly or spinning rig with bubble to retrieve a dark wet-fly a foot or two under the surface, usually with fair results. A pattern such as an Orange Asher will often bring good results. The bag will usually be a mixture of kokanee and any species of trout present, and will typically consist of more trout than kokanee.

At Williams Creek Reservoir, near Pagosa Springs, Colorado, kokanee are often found feeding alongside good-sized brook trout. Across the mountains to the east at Beaver Creek Reservoir, one will catch bluebacks and cutthroats. Be careful, once they find out how good kokanee taste, everyone in your camp will fight over the salmon and leave the trout for someone else.

Kokanee can be taken with flies in few places other than situations similar to those previously mentioned. One such exception is the Kootenai River. The best place for this is the pool right below Libby Dam near Libby, Montana in the northwest corner of the state. Here, kokanee, trout, and other species are constantly fed into the river below the dam though the turbines of the big hydropower operation there. Incredibly, a large percentage of these fish make the trip down through the power plant alive and well. Gradually, many migrate down the river if unmolested, but there is always a good population in the pool.

Fly fishing here for kokanee can be productive. Streamers work well as do small spinners. The pool and the river below are large enough to lend themselves to this kind of angling.

Fly-Fishing Equipment

As previously stated, kokanee like small fluorescent orange or chartreuse wet flies or egg imitations in the fall as the spawn is starting to roll. Small streamers may work then also.

In spring, when kokanee may be in the bays, try to match any hatch that comes along. A sinking nymph and floating line is often the ticket here, as it mimics well the nymphs that are ascending from the bottom to the surface.

Some anglers troll in open water with fly equipment in spring when the kokes are not too deep. This is typically done with sink tip lines and with around 15 feet of 4- to 8-pound mono leader. A small wedding ring spinner with a fly in place of the hook makes an effective and lightweight rig. One must often add sinkers to get the lure down to the kokes.

Section Four

4

KOKANEE SALMON MANAGEMENT

HATCHERY REPRODUCTION AND STOCKING

Ten

WHY KOKANEE ARE STOCKED

Popularity

"In most good kokanee waters, kokanee are the preferred fish even if rainbow trout actually compose the bulk of the fish harvested by anglers," says Patrick J. Martinez, Wildlife Researcher with the Colorado Division of Wildlife. Pat works extensively with kokanee and is a true expert. Another expert, Wade Fredenberg of Montana Game and Fish, feels that the kokanee is the most popular fish in northwestern Montana.

Larry Federici, Superintendent of Navajo Lake State Park in northern New Mexico and a well-known expert on the fish in that part of the world, has said that it is primarily the kokanee salmon that provides the revenue to keep Navajo Lake State Park open. Navajo is a fine lake for rainbow and brown trout, crappie, northern pike, channel cats, and largemouth and smallmouth bass. Among all these, the kokanee is king.

As a Food Fish

Kokanee are popular in part because they are among the best tasting of freshwater fish. Their flesh is deep pink/orange and rich. Broiled or cooked on a grill in foil, it is sweet and mild. Since I became addicted, a long stretch without kokanee in the summer or fall brings on severe withdrawal symptoms.

The kokanee feeds low on the food chain, and is short-lived. This means it does not accumulate pollutants in its tissue to the same degree as predatory fish or those that live longer. This is a legitimate concern in so many of our clear, cold mountain lakes in the West, some of which contain high concentrations of mercury and other potentially dangerous contaminants.

As a Sport Fish

In the past, bluebacks have had a reputation for not being great fighters because people pursued them with very heavy equipment. Lately, the increasing popularity of the downrigger has allowed more folks to fish with lighter equipment. On a light rig, a kokanee puts up an astonishing fight. It would be hard to name a freshwater fish that fights better, pound for pound.

In waters with good kokanee populations, angling probably has little impact on numbers of kokanee present. In Flaming Gorge Reservoir, Utah Fisheries Biologists have found that angler impact on kokanee is barely significant compared to the effects of predation by the laker trout.

On Navajo Lake in New Mexico, kokanee get a great deal of fishing pressure.

Catching kokanee makes people happy, as attested by the expression on the face of the author's son Jim as he shows off a nice 17-incher.

Yet each fall, many thousands of spawners show up in various sections of the lake. They are snagged by the hundreds and taken away and still thousands die naturally in the lake, unable to spawn successfully due to lack of proper habitat. The impact of taking home a limit, it seems, is virtually nil.

As Forage for Bigger Fish

Kokanee are stocked in some lakes primarily as food for larger game fish. The most common predators fed with kokanee are landlocked Chinook salmon and brown, rainbow, bull, and lake trout. Kokanee are perfect food for kings, Gerrard rainbows, and mackinaw because all these species are pelagic, frequenting open water. Kings, Gerrards, and mackinaw go with kokanee as stripers, wipers and white bass go with shad in warm waters.

The big Gerrard rainbows of Pend Oreille Lake in northern Idaho and other waters are famed for their astonishing fighting ability. They often exceed 20 pounds, and they reach this large size by munching on kokanee.

In Coeur d'Alene Lake in Idaho, the success of the chinook salmon is due largely to the presence of kokanee as ideal forage for the larger salmon. Many trophy lake trout fisheries owe their success to the kokanee.

As Competitors with Rough Fish

Kokanee are occasionally stocked to compete with "rough" fish. In Strawberry Reservoir, Utah biologists stocked kokanee for two reasons as part of a unique and brilliant plan for management of this unusually rich fishery.

The kokanee was stocked in Strawberry to act as abundant forage for an exceptionally predatory fish also stocked there, the Bear Lake cutthroat trout.

The kokanee was also established in Strawberry to compete with the Utah chub,

Given the way they fit harmlessly into many lakes, their fighting ability, and their great-tasting flesh, one has to conclude that kokanee ought to be introduced into more lakes every year.

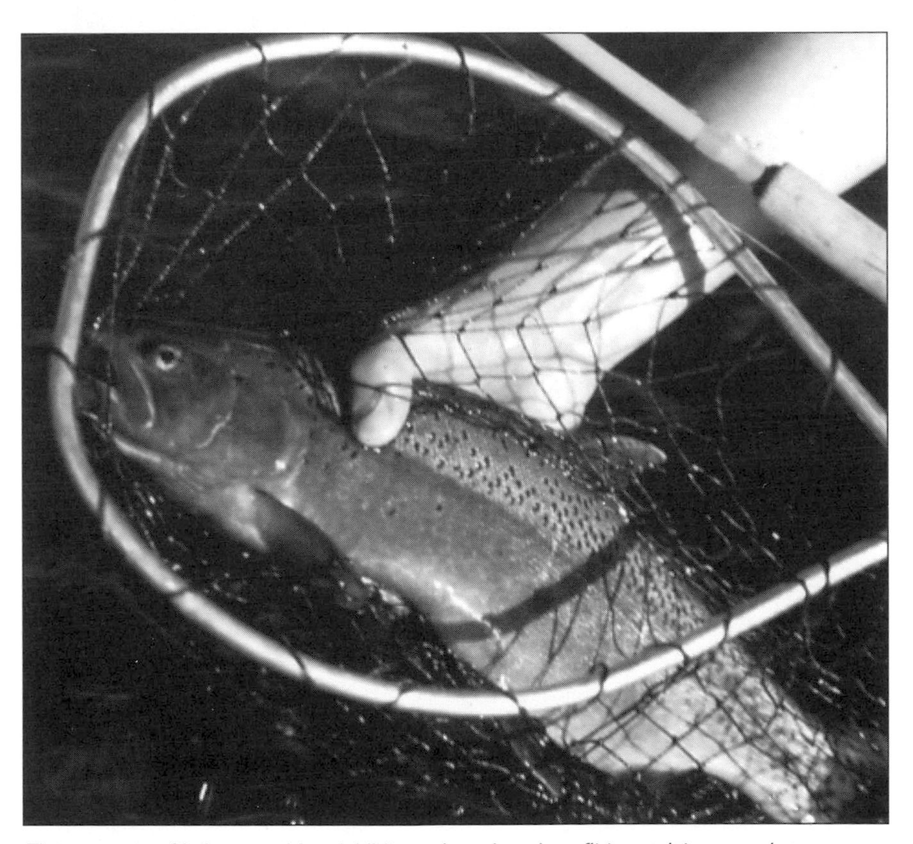

The presence of kokanee seldom inhibits and can be a benefit to predatory species.

Tim Barry, Connecticut Fisheries

Connecticut biologists pull a gill net used to catch spawning kokanee for egg and milt collection.

which, like the kokanee, feeds heavily on plankton. The chub and other rough fish took over that lake in the 1980s. The lake was treated with rotenone in 1990, the largest application of that South American poison to date. The treatment seems to have been very successful.

It is hoped that competition from the kokanee and predation from the cutthroats will make things tough enough on the remaining resident chubs and suckers to keep their numbers under control.

As Noncompetitive Additional Quarry for Anglers

Kokanee are planted to add another species to a lake in which they will do no harm to other populations of game fish. Sometimes the kokes are able to use a food source not already being used and improve the fishery at the same time.

Kokanee are growing well in McPhee Reservoir in southwestern Colorado. They are feeding on planktonic organisms too small for rainbows to use. They are in fact doing better than the rainbows in McPhee, and will probably become more important to area anglers as folks catch on. Plans are in the making to have McPhee become another kokanee egg source for Colorado.

ARTIFICIALLY ENHANCED REPRODUCTION

Kokanee Egg Production

Most hatcheries do not raise kokanee brood stock as they often do trout. Since the fish are only good for one spawn, such a practice would not be economical. Instead, they catch spawning kokanee from tributaries of certain lakes, take eggs and milt from them, fertilize and incubate the eggs, and raise the fry to any of various sizes in a hatchery.

There is an exception to this, however, and it is working surprisingly well. At Creston Hatchery, Montana fisheries personnel are holding brood-size kokanee and spawning them. They feed these fish on prepared meal which has no crustaceans in it, so the kokes do not turn red or orange when they spawn. The fisheries technicians worried about this at first, but the eggs are turning out fine. They are showing an excellent survival rate in the area of 95 percent.

The eggs of these crustacean-free kokanee are bright yellow, and the folks who work with them have been calling them "kokanee gold." The fish that come from these eggs, once in the lake and on the usual diet of Daphnia and other crustaceans, will have orange or pink flesh and will color up at spawn like any other wild kokanee.

Actually, kokanee in different places vary greatly in color at spawning. The degree to which they turn red or produce pink or orange flesh depends on their diet in the wild also. The same is true of other salmonids.

Colorado currently produces and exports many millions of eggs per year; Oregon often has surplus eggs. In the East, Connecticut provides eggs for itself and for New York. Utah is working on becoming an egg provider. Many states need more than they can produce and are constantly on the lookout for sources.

California, a "Special Case"

With its huge human population and exorbitant taxes, one would think the Golden State would have money to burn. But California's Department of Fish & Game seems to have a money shortage and an overabundance of incompetent administrators.

The California Fisheries personnel I have dealt with are as dedicated, honest, and competent as those of any other state. But I have dealt primarily with biologists who are in their line of work because they love it and because they want to do something good.

The problem rests with the folks holding the higher positions in the administration. California has closed Fish & Game offices that should not have been closed, effectively withdrawing services from areas that need them.

One notable area so neglected is the Tahoe Basin. This is one of California's most actively fished areas. It had one of the more competent and dedicated fisheries biologists in the nation. But the Department of Fish & Game administrators demonstrated that combination of arrogance and ignorance so typical of corporate and government leadership, and shipped him out.

California put an end to its kokanee stocking program in the late 1980s and early 1990s. In spite of the fact that the state has many lakes that are ideal kokanee habitat, and that the fish is quite popular there, the administration snuffed their kokanee program. California would not have kokanee if it were not for a private organization called The California Inland Fisheries Foundation and its Project Kokanee.

Led by a handful of dedicated anglers, Project Kokanee donates thousands of dollars and hundreds of man-hours of volunteer labor yearly to the kokanee cause. Producing and procuring around 1.8 million fry per year and distributing them to

Dana Dewey and Roger Wilson, Utah Game & Fish

A Utah worker strips eggs from a big hen at the egg collecting facility on the Strawberry River.

the various suitable waters, Project Kokanee has kept the kokanee program alive and well in California. Project Kokanee can be reached at P.O. Box 188739, Sacramento, CA 95818-8739, 916/456-5981.

Much has improved in California in the last two years. Some of the old administrators have retired or are soon to retire, and new people are being brought in to replace them. In general, things are looking up.

Harvesting Eggs

Kokanee are caught during the spawn, the eggs and milt taken from them, and then they are allowed to go free or are otherwise disposed of. Sometimes they are given to people who are visiting the hatchery or spawning site.

Some fisheries departments have facilities where the kokes come almost to the hatchery to spawn. Probably the most successful of these operations is the Roaring Judy Hatchery in Colorado. The kokanee from which the Roaring Judy personnel take eggs and milt journey about 25 miles from Blue Mesa Reservoir to the hatchery. Having been reared in and set free near the hatchery, it is natural that they imprint on the hatchery water and return to the hatchery to spawn.

In some cases it is deemed necessary to imprint the kokanee with the scent of a chemical reagent to get them to return to a desired area for the spawn. Several hundred yards up the Strawberry River from Strawberry Reservoir in central Utah is a new egg-taking facility that belongs to the Utah Department of Game and Fish. To assure that spawning kokanee will return up the Strawberry River to the facility when their time comes, fingerlings are imprinted with morpholine. A small amount of morpholine, a compound often used to control pH in water, is added to their water when the fry are developing, and the fish imprint the aroma of that bad-smelling amine into their brains.

Tim Barry, Connecticut Fisheries

As eggs are collected, milt is mixed in with them. This salmon lived its life in Connecticut.

Near spawning time each year, a small amount of morpholine is drip fed into the Strawberry River above the facility to call the spawners back. They can detect the reagent in very low concentrations, so not enough morpholine is added to the river and reservoir to do any harm as a pollutant.

Imprinting is not usually necessary where the hatchery and egg-taking facility are in the same place. If the hatchery is right there, as at Roaring Judy, the kokes simply imprint on the chemistry of the hatchery water and come back upstream to that. At Strawberry, the hatcheries that raise the fingerlings are miles away in other watersheds, thus the necessity to imprint.

New Mexico is starting what should turn out to be a superb egg-producing program on the Chama River above El Vado Lake. This should be a model program when it reaches its full production potential. New Mexico biologists are setting up an egg-taking operation downstream from the Parkview Hatchery, were many of New Mexico's kokanee are raised. The water from the hatchery empties into the Chama and flows with the river out into El Vado Lake, where these particular kokanee will live their lives. The unique chemistry of the hatchery water will call the spawners back when the time comes.

For catching kokanee in a stream up which they run to spawn, a fence is often constructed across the stream. Somewhere in the fence is the notch or weir through which kokes can swim. The kokanee, highly motivated to go upstream, finds his or her way up through the notch. Sometimes the way leads into a fish trap that accumulates and holds the fish. In other cases, the fence inhibits travel back downstream, and the kokes just congregate in a hole above the fence.

Kokanee are occasionally caught in lakes or streams by electroshocking and then netting the stunned fish. There is some controversy about the survival rate of the eggs from parents that were electroshocked, but nothing conclusive has been found to date. Studies continue, one of the most aggressive being conducted on Heron Lake by Greg Friday of New Mexico Game & Fish. Trapped kokanee are sorted to find those that are ready to spawn. Those that are not are put back into holding pens to wait. Ripe fish are taken to the spawning facility and put into a holding tank there. Usually, males and females are put in separate tanks.

The spawning facility may be a temporary or permanent structure. It usually consists of some type of holding tanks for male and female fish, metal tables on which to work, and if the facility is outside, a source of shade, as sun will kill eggs or sperm in a few minutes.

Each fish is held gently over a pan. The worker runs his thumb and fingers back along the fish's belly, squeezing gently from either side, and forcing eggs or milt out into the pan.

Females are taken one at a time and the eggs squeezed from them into the pan. Milt from the males is emptied into the same pan with the eggs and these are mixed around gently. Quite often, more than one worker will be putting eggs and milt into the same pan. Sperm and eggs from many fish are accumulated in the pan in a ratio of about 10 females to every seven males. Soon the eggs and milt are mixed and emptied into a larger container.

The egg has a small pore in the membrane called a micropyle. Its function is to admit one sperm cell into the egg. As soon as a sperm cell enters, or in any case after about three minutes, the micropyle closes.

Sperm cells have a very short life span. They typically last 45 to 60 seconds in the water. By adding a weak solution of pure sodium chloride (0.0038 grams of NaCl per gallon of water) the sperm can be helped to live up to three minutes. Sperm life span can be increased to five minutes by adding a solution of one packet per liter of water of a French product called Dilueur 532. Some states use it; many do not, feeling they get adequate fertilization without it.

Once the eggs are fertilized, they are allowed to harden in cold water for an hour before any attempt is made to transport them. This water hardening makes them much tougher than they would be otherwise. They can easily be shipped during the first 12 hours after water hardening. After the initial 12 hours, the eggs have to wait for eye-up in about 35 days to be tough enough for any further moving.

In the Hatchery

When water-hardened eggs arrive at the hatchery, they are usually disinfected with Argentyne or Betadyne, depending on their source. Eggs can be so disinfected without harm, fry cannot. Workers are more likely to disinfect eggs that have come from waters other than their own.

Next the eggs are put into an incubator. Other than treating them about 15 minutes per day with a 1600 PPM solution of Formalin to kill fungus, they are left alone.

Eye-up is the time in the development of the egg when you can look at the egg and actually see the eye of the little varmint inside. Eye-up is significant, because from that point until hatching, eggs are rather tough and can be shipped all over the country by being packed in wet cheesecloth.

Eye-up occurs in about 32 to 35 days in 48 degree water, faster if the water is warmer and slower in colder water. After eye-up, the eggs are put on a screen and physically shocked by jarring the screen on a table. The eggs that are not viable will become opaque after this process and can be sorted out by an electronic egg sorter. (The job can be done by hand, but is very time consuming; the sorter is capable of sorting about 100,000 eggs per hour.) Total time to hatching is about 60 to 65 days, depending largely on water temperature.

Once eggs are hatched, they are moved to the hatchery room or building, put in troughs through which fresh water runs, and covered to protect them from light. They are kept there until swim-up, when the fry have absorbed their yolk sacks and are off the bottom and swimming around. Swim-up in kokanee typically occurs about a month after hatching. From this point on, they are fed commercial fish food until they are transported and stocked.

Whirling Disease

You have no doubt heard about whirling disease. It is a malady that attacks young salmonids, causing them to swim in circles as if chasing their tails. It also causes death or deformities and leaves the young fish very vulnerable to predation.

Kokanee were thought to be immune to whirling disease, but it has recently been found in this fish. How seriously it will impact the kokanee and how far it will spread remains to be seen. The fact the kokes can get the disease is not good news, however.

Planting Size

The size to which young kokanee are raised before being planted depends largely on hatchery space available. It is becoming more and more evident that the young koke's chance to survive in the wild increases with age at planting. Also, kokanee taken in winter and raised until late spring when plankton is abundant will be released into a more food-rich environment than fry released into relatively plankton-poor winter waters.

The size of fry is often measured by the number of fish it takes to weigh a pound. Sizes commonly stocked range from recently hatched fry at around 4000 fish-per-pound to "catchables" at 10 per pound. Newly hatched fish in the 5000 fish per pound range are classed as sac fry. They are called fry from swim-up until they reach the size at which it takes about 1000 of them to weigh a pound. At that point, when they are about an inch and a half in length, the young fish are usually called advanced fry. Fish in the two- to three-inch range (300-400 per pound) are fingerlings, and sub-catchables are in the six- to seven-inch range and up. Eight-inch fish are considered catchables.

Some studies indicate that kokanee in the advanced fry stage are at the ideal size for stocking, based on the economics of growing them and the expected rate of survival. Many states hold them longer, however, willing to spend extra money to assure a greater survival rate.

It is this 1000 fish-per-pound size that many hatcheries are shooting for, though limited hatchery space and the need to grow other species can force earlier stocking. Earlier stockings are usually somewhat successful, but survival rate is typically better if the little guys are allowed to reach the 1000-per-pound size or larger and are released into the plankton-rich waters of spring.

HAZARDS TO LIFE AND FIN

BAD TIMING ON THE PLANT

A lake is not a friendly place to a small fish. The main problem is that everyone out there wants to eat you. Fisheries personnel who introduce fingerlings into lakes have some control over just how unfriendly the little fish's new home is when he or she gets there.

In a certain lake in a certain Western state, a large state division of fisheries planting of kokanee fry followed by only a day, a large planting of catchable (six- to eight-inch) rainbow trout by the U.S. Fish and Wildlife Service. The result? Very fat and happy rainbows and a very low kokanee survival rate.

Both plantings took place in the same location; the rainbows were still hanging around, not having dispersed into the lake yet. They were grateful for all the tiny snacks poured in for their eating pleasure. The kokanee were less happy about the whole thing, but their cries of protest were soon silenced.

PREDATION/COMPETITION

Lake trout are voracious predators. They are all the more dangerous to kokanee because the two species tend to hang out in much the same habitat. Mackinaw, often with the help of the small shrimp *Mysis relicta*, have been at least partially to blame for the collapse of several kokanee populations. It is difficult to determine how much at fault the mackinaw or the *Mysis* really is, however, because it seems there are always other factors at work.

Priest Lake in northern Idaho is a prime example. It was once a choice kokanee fishery and still holds the Idaho state record. Mackinaw were already in the lake when kokanee were introduced. *Mysis* are present in the lake also. As the kokanee came on, the lakers did also, and predation became more and more prevalent. At about the same time, a dam was built and used to bring the lake level up about three feet. The level was raised and lowered periodically. Sometime later the kokanee population collapsed.

Did the kokanee die off because of competition with the shrimp? Because of the shrimp serving to feed immature lakers and bring them more quickly to a size at which they were able to eat kokanee? Because the raising and lowering of the lake level interfered with the kokanee's ability to spawn successfully? No one knows for sure.

Priest now has a population of mackinaw that live primarily on opossum shrimp and smaller mackinaw. There are a few old bull trout in there that are too big and mean and tough for the mackinaw to eat. Kokes are few or none.

Probably the most tragic of all kokanee horror stories took place in Flathead

Lake, Montana. Flathead is, at about 128,000 surface acres, big enough to make it the largest natural freshwater lake in the western United States.

It is a good place to fish, trophy lakers being the prime draw. Several species of whitefish, those seriously underrated relatives of trout, live here. There are a few cutthroats. Flathead was, up until the mid-1980s, one of the finest kokanee fisheries anywhere.

Kokanee were introduced into Flathead in 1916. It took them some time to establish good populations in the big lake; it took a while longer for them to be discovered as the wonderful sport and food fish they are. By the 1930s, kokanee were abundant and popular.

In 1937, the Kerr Dam was built below the outlet of Flathead Lake, and power production caused drawdowns. The resulting fluctuation of water levels may have exposed kokanee redds and killed many eggs. But the fabulous kokanee fishery persisted, its popularity grew.

In 1952, the Bureau of Reclamation built the Hungry Horse Dam on the South Fork of the Flathead River. Fluctuating flows in that stream then caused increased mortality of kokanee eggs in the South Fork every year.

Mysis relicta were brought from Waterton Lake, where they are naturally abundant, and released in Swan, Whitefish, and Ashley lakes in 1968 and 1975.

Since the water of all these lakes eventually goes through Flathead, it was not long until *Mysis* relicta made its debut in the big lake. The first specimens were collected there in 1981. *Mysis* densities grew from barely detectable in 1981 to a lakewide average of 45 individuals per square meter of surface water in 1985.

The impact of the shrimp on *Daphnia* populations was soon evident. Densities of *Daphnia thorata* in Flathead ran in the neighborhood of 3 to 4.5 organisms per liter between 1980 and 1982. Each year, the little crustacean had shown up in detectable numbers by April, with significant population pulses achieved by late May. By 1987, populations were lower than one organism per liter. *Daphnia thorata* were not present in the spring of 1987 in detectable quantities until late May. Small population pulses occurred that year, but not until July.

Kokanee survival from fry to adult was about 3 percent from 1981 to 1985. It dropped to 0.7 percent in 1986 and to 0.01 percent in 1987. The kokanee harvest dropped from over 200,000 fish per year to virtually nothing after 1985.

Ron Raiha of Sandpoint, Idaho tells of loading up carloads of anglers in Sandpoint on Pend Oreille Lake to make the long drive to Flathead in the 70s to fish for kokanee. He describes big catches of kokanee that averaged nearly two feet long (measuring with his hands). But the fishing ended in the mid-80s, and everyone quit going.

One favorite kokanee spawning stream was McDonald Creek, a short tributary of the Middle Fork of the Flathead River. The creek comes from Lake McDonald and for most of its length is situated on land administered by Glacier National Park. Between 1979 and 1985, from 26,000 to 118,000 kokanee spawned in the little stream per year. In 1987, 330 showed up and in 1989, 50. As the kokanee disappeared from McDonald Creek, so did the birds.

What birds? Why, the bald eagles that came each fall to eat spawning, dying, and dead salmon. Thirty-seven eagles showed up in 1939 to munch on kokanee. In 1981, 639 eagles were counted in one canoe trip on McDonald, as were over

100,000 spawning salmon.

McDonald became the sight of the densest concentrations of bald eagles south of Canada. In 1983, 46,500 viewers came to the visitor's center on McDonald Creek to watch the eagles. A total of 25 eagles were counted in the whole fall of 1989 and fewer than 1,000 viewers showed.

Anglers that had been catching over 100,000 spawning kokanee per year caught less than 6000 in 1987 and none since then. One of Montana's most popular fisheries was obliterated.

The Montana fisheries folk have dumped an unprecedented number of kokanee fry into Flathead in the last several years in an attempt to get the fish established again. To date, with the investment running up around $2 million, nothing has worked. Though kokes are present in some of the smaller lakes on Flathead's tributaries, few to none are able to live in the big lake.

Terry Wygart, Colorado Division of Wildlife

Mysis relicta.

THE *MYSIS* HAZARD

The most ironic part of all this is that *Mysis* were planted in many lakes as food for kokanee. Biologists originally thought that to plant *Mysis* in a lake was to encourage the growth of hugc kokanee in the six-pound range. It seemed so because of the experience of British Columbia biologists with the West Arm of Kootenay Lake.

Kootenay Lake is located in southeastern British Columbia. It is an ocean by the standards of many lake anglers in the United States. Water flows into this huge lake from various sources, including the Kootenay River, and out through the West Arm of the lake.

Mysis relicta was introduced into Kootenay and several other B.C. lakes in the mid-1960s as extra forage for kokanee and other species. In most situations, *Mysis* does the kokanee little or no good, as we have seen.

Where the waters of Kootenay Lake funnel into the West Arm on their way to the outlet, the bottom comes up and there is a washing up of things from the depths of the main lake into the upper waters of the West Arm. Among the things washing up from those depths are thousands of *Mysis relicta*, which the hungry West Arm kokanee gratefully welcome with open mouth.

Following the introduction of opossum shrimp to the lake, the West Arm of Kootenay began producing six-pound kokanee in good numbers. The fame of this fishery spread far and wide, not escaping the attention of biologists interested in improving kokanee fisheries in other waters. Introducing *Mysis relicta* into kokanee lakes in an effort to grow big kokes became the thing to do.

Thus many lakes, particularly those with lakers present, lost their kokanee populations entirely, while many others saw severe declines in kokanee size and abundance. The little *Mysis* is with us to this day.

MYSIS EATERS

In talking about living organisms, words like "typically," "usually," and "virtually" pop up with great regularity. This is because just when you think you have something figured out, along comes a case that refutes all you thought you knew. So we say the *Mysis* shrimp "typically" or "usually" has a negative impact on kokanee. But there are kokanee that appear to be actively feeding on *Mysis* shrimp.

In Wallowa Lake in eastern Oregon, biologist Bill Knox tells me that the opossum shrimp may be having a positive impact on kokanee. He says further studies are necessary to be sure, but that appears to be the case. I am told also that kokanee seem to be munching *Mysis* in Lake Tahoe. Tahoe, a sterile lake, does seem to be growing some awfully big kokanee recently.

The best documentation so far of this shrimp-eating behavior in kokanee seems to be the case of Swan Lake, in western Montana. There, I am told by biologist Jim Vashro, one catches two distinct sizes of kokanee salmon from two different groups. If you troll at, say, 30 feet, you catch small kokes in the pound range. They are your typical, run-of-the-mill kokes that eat primarily *Daphnia*. But drop down and drag your lure just off the bottom and you begin catching big, deep-bodied, orange-fleshed three-pounders.

This is also seen when biologists catch Swan kokanee for the spawn. Approximately 3 percent of the kokanee are considerably larger than the norm in Swan.

HUMAN FACTORS

As we shall see, many of the instances in which kokanee populations crashed involved more than just the opossum shrimp and the mackinaw. Typically that "more" was the two-legged tool maker and his never-ending need to mess with things.

Sometimes, unknown to those in charge, water chemistry is changed. A lake is much more than a big puddle of water; it is a deceptively complex ecosystem. When a significant event—good or bad—occurs in a lake, the cause is often much more difficult to understand than one might suppose.

The evidence on Flathead and Priest lakes points nearly as much toward dams as toward shrimp and mackinaw as the cause of the drastic declines in kokanee numbers. Changing lake levels, especially having the lake at the wrong level in the fall, or suddenly dropping that level, can wreak havoc on kokanee spawning redds.

Koocanusa is one of the potentially great kokanee lakes in the world. Though severely affected by drawdown for a part of each year, it is a quality late-summer fishery.

Kootenay Lake, far to the northwest, is the home of a unique strain of rainbow trout—the largest and fiercest strain in the world—the Gerrard rainbow. The trout developed here, some say, from ancient steelhead stock that came here when Kootenay had more direct connections to the ocean. Be that as it may, the Gerrard is ferociously piscivorous and one of the greatest fighters in all of freshwater fishing. It loves kokanee salmon.

Gerrards first spawn when they are four years old, and then they spawn in spring. Kootenay Lake has few streams that are clear enough in the spring to support a spawn. The only places the Gerrards have historically had to spawn were the

Ron Carey

A fat Flaming Gorge female. So this is what all the fuss is about.

Lardeau and Duncan rivers downstream from small lakes that acted as filters, cleaning the spring runoff water of its silt. Below each of the two small lakes in these two rivers are short stretches where gravel stays clean enough to allow the big rainbows to spawn successfully. Thus two varieties of the Gerrard strain developed, one that spawned in each river.

This limitation of spawning sites prohibited the majority of rainbows from spawning in any given year. This, and the large size of the gravel in the spawning areas, created a naturally selective pressure that favored the largest, strongest, and most aggressive trout. Only they were allowed to pass on their genetic traits. This may be much of the cause for the Gerrard rainbow's huge size and ferocious nature.

In a stroke of genius typical of our species, some member of the Canadian government decided to build a dam across the Duncan River. This dam condemned to extinction the population of rainbows that had spawned in the Duncan. Some of the fish were taken to a national fish hatchery in Montana in an attempt to save them, but budget cutbacks designed to pad the salaries of high-level bureaucrats curtailed activities at the hatchery and terminated the Duncan strain of the Gerrard rainbow.

But the Duncan Dam may well have had a broader effect on Kootenay Lake. One of Kootenay Lake's major sources of nutrients seems to have been the Duncan River. Duncan Dam, like most dams, acted as a settling and reaction pond, taking most of these good chemicals out of the water before they reached the lake.

Occasionally when we humans impact one system, our influencing of another covers up our original mistake, at least for a time. Thus it was when Consolidated Mining and Smelting opened a fertilizer plant far up the Kootenai River.

Kootenai River is roughly shaped like the letter "U." The right arm of the U drops down out of Canada and makes a curve to the west at about Libby Dam. The bottom of the U heads west through the northwest corner of Montana past the towns of Libby and Troy, and into northern Idaho. The left or west arm of the U then juts north, back into Canada, ending at Kootenay Lake. CM&S's fertilizer plant is way over on the right or east arm of the "U."

Pollution in the form of phosphate compounds from the fertilizer plant was carried by the Kootenai River around the bottom of the U and into Kootenay Lake. This accidental donation of nutritional treasures from afar more than negated whatever bad effects the damming of the Duncan River had had on the supply of nutrients to the lake.

If only we could quit when we were ahead. We had screwed up, only to be saved by another screw-up. But then some engineer in an office in Washington or Ottawa or Calgary or Missoula decided, "Let's build a dam across the Kootenay River above Libby. That ought to preserve our useless existence for another decade until retirement comes along." Thus came screw-up number three, Libby Dam.

As with every other dam on every other stream in the world, Lake Koocanusa acted as a place for chemical reactions and as a settling pond; most of the desperately needed phosphate stayed therein. To its credit, Koocanusa, with all that phosphate, grows fat kokanee and healthy fish of other species. But Kootenay Lake, its kokanee, its big bright bull trout, its many other species of fish, and its famous, beautiful, huge, wonderfully unique and fierce Gerrard rainbows are again being cheated of the nutrition they need.

There has been talk of artificial fertilization of Kootenay Lake. If one considers the size of Kootenay, the size of such an undertaking makes prospects for success seem remote.

ILLEGALLY AND ACCIDENTALLY INTRODUCED SPECIES

Illegally introduced species have ruined many kokanee and trout populations. Some of the worst are rough fish such as chubs, yellow perch, alewives, and predators such as lakers, walleyes and northern pike.

All else being well, the salmonids can live with any of these fish, but if something puts the kokes or trout at a disadvantage, the population may be obliterated.

FUTURE OF THE KOKANEE

Despite the hazards and accidents, the future of the kokanee appears bright in most states. The fish is becoming so popular that state agencies are responding to public demand and are improving their kokanee programs to provide the fish the people want. Hatchery production is being stepped up. More studies are being done to learn how to grow kokanee bigger and in larger numbers, and to avoid conditions that have destroyed populations in the past. In some areas, the koke is being introduced into new waters. It looks like ol' blueback just might be around for a long, long time.

Section Five

PLACES

Twelve

COMMENTS ON A FEW GOOD LAKES

BRITISH COLUMBIA

Osoyoos Lake

One does not think of Canada as a land of deserts or warm-water lakes, but Osoyoos, lying on the border of B.C. and Washington State, challenges that perception. The area surrounding the lake boasts several species not ordinarily thought of as Canadian, including burrowing owls, horned lizards, scorpions, and painted turtles.

In addition to kokanee in good numbers, the lake holds largemouth bass, perch, crappie. There are also rainbows up to 10 pounds.

CALIFORNIA

Don Pedro

Built in 1971, Don Pedro is probably the best kokanee lake in California, a state that is rich in kokanee lakes. In August, the angler can expect to catch good numbers of two-and three-pounders, with fish of over four pounds showing up occasionally.

Safely in the net. A net is essential in boating kokanee, as this lightly hooked Koocanusa individual demonstrates.

Boca

Boca is a very good kokanee lake, producing kokanee in the 18- to 19-inch range in late summer. Boca is only two miles from Stampede, another fine kokanee water with bluebacks up to about 16 inches.

Bullard's Bar

The Bar has kokes in abundance, but they run small due to their huge numbers. This may be intentional; there is something to be said for managing some waters for large numbers of fish instead of large fish. Many anglers are overjoyed with abundant catches of tasty salmon in the 12-inch range.

The best part of this lake for kokes is the main body above the dam to points upstream just above the forks. This is also a decent bass, trout, and catfish lake.

Tahoe

Tahoe is situated on the border of California and Nevada. It is the home to native Lahonton cutthroats, lake trout, rainbow and brown trout, kokanee salmon and *Mysis relicta.* The mackinaw is quite popular here.

As a kokanee water, Tahoe is a sleeper. Tahoe gave up some 24-inch kokes in late summer 1995, with more expected in 1996. Good kokanee spots include the area around the mouth of the Truckee River, Meeks Bay, and much of the south quarter of the lake.

COLORADO

Eleven Mile

Eleven Mile, located about 40 miles west of Colorado Springs on the South Platte River, is a good lake for huge kokanee, rainbows, browns, and northern pike. This little body of water produces some of the biggest kokes to be found anywhere. Kokes of 20 inches are not uncommon, and six-pounders do occur.

I talked to Chris Holm of Eleven Mile State Park and Biologist Gregg Pataski of the Colorado Division of Wildlife in July 1996. Good numbers of kokanee in the 16-inch range were being taken, with about one out of five going over 20 inches. I asked Gregg if there was anything he would like the reader to know about Eleven Mile. He asked me to encourage everyone to catch and keep northern pike.

For more information, call or write Eleven Mile State Park, 4229 County Road 92, Lake George, CO 80827, 719/748-3401.

Blue Mesa

This is Colorado's largest impoundment, the home of the famous kokanee that make the run each year to the Roaring Judy Hatchery. Blue Mesa is acclaimed as the state's best kokanee water and its largest source of kokanee eggs. It is probably the largest source of kokanee eggs in the world.

The Elk Creek Marina can supply you with boats, information, tackle, supplies, and food. Call Carole at 970/641-0707.

McPhee

A regular kokanee stocking program was initiated on McPhee in 1991. This program has been quite successful. McPhee has considerable small zooplankton,

This koke, though nice, is not a big one in Eleven Mile, west of Colorado Springs.

which the rainbow trout and other species present in the lake hardly use. Kokanee are able to do well on this resource.

Mike Japhet, Colorado DOW aquatic biologist responsible for most of southwestern Colorado, is hoping to make McPhee another source for kokanee eggs in the future. McPhee promises to be a very good kokanee lake.

As I talked to the folks at McPhee Marina in July 1996, kokes were suspended at about 40 feet. Many were being caught in the 14-inch range. In addition to the kokes, McPhee provides very good fishing for smallmouths, channel cats, trout, and panfish.

For more information, contact McPhee Marina at 970/882-2257.

CONNECTICUT

Lakeville Lake or Wonoskopomuc (its older name) is the egg source for Connecticut as well as for New York State. It has a good population of foot-long kokanee, so far. This is the hangout of Frank Verano, who has taught scores of people to catch this delightful fish.

West Hill Pond is similar to Lakeville Lake where kokanee are concerned. It has a stable population of small to medium kokanee.

East Twin Lake is a little bigger at 562 acres and is deep for its size at over 700 feet. This was once the premier Connecticut kokanee lake. It produced larger kokanee in good numbers. Then someone illegally introduced the alewife into the lake. The alewife is a voracious plankton eater, and it ate the kokanee out of house and home.

For more information, call the Connecticut fisheries people at 860/424-3011.

GLACIER NATIONAL PARK

While this beautiful park has several lakes with kokanee in them, they are not what most kokanee anglers would call kokanee lakes. The lakes are clear, cold, oligotrophic. The kokanee are small. In many cases, there is no way to get a boat on the water, no way to troll. If you are packing in with a float tube or little raft to fish for cutthroats or bull trout, you can try for them if you want.

Glacier is a dazzling place to spend time. The scenery is magnificent, the wildlife plentiful and fascinating.

IDAHO

Pend Orielle

"Ponderay" is the biggest lake in Idaho. It is one of the biggest natural freshwater lakes in the western U.S. Flathead and Tahoe are bigger, few others. This is deep water at around 1200 feet. It is used to train U.S. Navy personnel who will work on submarines.

Pend Oreille has good cutthroat fisheries here and there all around the lake. Here is one of the better populations of the great Gerrard Rainbow in the world.

Kokanee are in good supply in Pend Oreille. Many forces are working against them, however. Many feel the lake is gradually losing its kokanee fishery.

In the earlier decades of this century, this lake produced tons of whitefish that were smoked here and shipped all over the country. The whitefish kept the area alive during the Great Depression.

A few folks still appreciate this underutilized fish. One such person is Ron Raiha, former owner of Pend Oreille Sports Shop in Sandpoint. One of Ron's boats is a little V-bottom that he rows out across the giant lake in the winter. Then he proceeds to fill his boat with whitefish using only a handline and a piece of red yarn on a hook.

The whitefish take the yarn hook very lightly. An experienced angler can fill his boat while a novice sits nearby, catching nothing but a cold.

Ron is a master at this game. He is also very knowledgeable about fish and game of all kinds in the Northwest. If you are going into the area to fish or hunt, stop in Sandpoint; pick up your equipment and supplies and the best information available anywhere at Pend Oreille Sports.

Coeur d'Alene

Fishing for kokes here picks up in early July, when they are typically about nine inches long. By late summer, they have usually reached 11 inches. Some hot spots include the Conklin area, Spokane Point, Windy Bay, and Wolf Lodge Bay.

The big draw here is the Chinook salmon, which grows well primarily due to the kokanee. For information, stop by Fins & Feathers Sports Shop in the town of Coeur d'Alene. Idaho Fish and Game also has an office in this town. Their number is 208/769-1414.

Dworshak

Dworshak is a major source for kokanee eggs in Idaho. Dworshak's ability to produce kokanee has been inhibited in the last few years by efforts to save the anadromous Pacific Salmon. Massive quantities of water have been let go to wash smolts downstream and the kokes have suffered.

Idaho's Fish & Game Department estimates a 90 percent drop in the Dworshak kokanee population during the March and April 1996 flushing. The population estimate for Dworshak stood at 150,000 in late April of 1996, as opposed to 1,300,000 before the flushing. The projection for 1997 is that there will be 40,000 mature kokanee in the reservoir. For information, visit the Riverside Husky Sports Shop in Orofino (208/476-5418).

Ron Carey

This big male is starting into the change that will prepare him for the spawn, and death.

MONTANA

Georgetown

Like many fertile lakes, Georgetown could have huge kokanee if it didn't have so many. But Georgetown has many underwater springs, in the gravel of which the kokes spawn. And though tributaries have been blocked to inhibit the kokanee spawn, the springs cannot be. So there are more mouths than groceries.

Under the good direction of biologist Wayne Hadley, the kokes at Georgetown are growing larger. At one time, they were so numerous that even the trout were stunting. Now the trout are bigger and the kokanee are decent size. A mature koke here now is around a foot long or a tad better.

Trolling in Georgetown is difficult at best. There is too much rooted aquatic vegetation. The best way to catch these sweet-fleshed little silvers is by jigging or fishing with bait.

Hauser

John Skibsrud of Deer Lodge is one fine night fisherman. He takes a lot of kokes from Hauser and other local lakes, the majority of them at night. The technique, discussed elsewhere, is much like the stillfishing described at Georgetown.

Hauser harbors some of the largest kokes in Montana. A photo John sent me of part of one night's catch shows several kokes that appear to be over three pounds.

For more information, call the Montana fisheries folks at 406/444-2535.

Koocanusa and the Kootenai River

Yea, it's a combined acronym—"Koo" for Kootenai, "can" for Canada, and "usa" for U.S.A. Clever, huh? It probably took a team of from 50 bureaucrats two years to come up with that name. Cost to the taxpayer was probably about $10 million.

Koocanusa is a fine kokanee lake. It also produces nice rainbows, cutts, ling or burbot, whitefish, and bull trout, those big cousins of the brookie.

Kokes, which were accidently introduced from farther upstream, run 10 to 13 inches, depending on population density and time of year. They are fat and full of fight. Kokes seem more abundant down near the dam end of the lake.

The lake has a serious drawdown problem. Check for water level before going there to fish.

The Corps of Engineers, ever fidgeting, sweating, wringing its hands, always looking for something beautiful to destroy, wants to dam the river again at Kootenai Falls. They really would like to build two more dams, the first being just below Libby Dam.

Why? One look at Kootenai Falls or the river above and below will tell you that this is a natural phenomenon far too wild and splendid to be tolerated by a bureaucrat, developer, industrialist, or politician.

Little Bitterroot

Here is some of the better kokanee fishing around, though the kokanee average only about 11 inches. A larger silver—16 to 20 inches—is caught occasionally.

Montana introduced Girrard rainbows in 1988. These members of the largest and most aggressive strain of rainbow trout are getting big. Fisheries personnel weighed 11 rainbows in the summer of 1995 in the 20- to 27-pound range. There are some cutthroat/rainbow hybrids in the 10- to 18-pound range.

Mary Ronan

Mary Ronan is home to rainbows, kokanee, cutts, and largemouth. The kokanee is the most sought-after species, accounting for 97 to 98 percent of angler hours. Biologist Wade Fredenberg of Kallispell feels that kokanee are the most sought after game fish in northwestern Montana.

Trolling or jigging around 40 feet in midsummer is productive just about

A great blue heron stands atop the cliffs by the Narrows on Heron Lake, as if guarding his namesake.

anywhere in the main body of the lake. Ice fishing is extremely popular here, and there is a fall snagging season for spawning kokes. The lake is closed for several weeks in spring in deference to the spawn of the self-sustaining rainbow population.

Illegally introduced in 1992, yellow perch have boomed here. In fall of 1995, two trap nets were set for kokanee spawn taking. In four weeks the nets caught 62,000 four to six-inch yellow perch. This could mean trouble.

NEW MEXICO

Eagle Nest

Eagle Nest is quite fertile, unusual for a cold water lake in New Mexico. It holds good populations of kokanee, rainbows, and cutthroats. This is one of the best cold water fisheries in New Mexico. The lake holds bizillions of white suckers.

If you are a kokanee fisherman and are in northeastern New Mexico, Eagle Nest would be a good place to stop. Contact Dos Amigos Trading Company at 505/377-6226 or Eagle Nest Marina at 505/377-6941.

Heron Lake

Heron is probably the southernmost lake in the country that holds lake trout. It also has good populations of rainbow and kokanee, and perhaps a few browns.

One of Heron's most attractive features is the "no-wake" rule in force there. Fishing on this lake is peaceful for that reason.

Kokanee grow well in Heron, and are typically around 17 to 18 inches by late summer. They spawn here in October through late December.

For more information, contact Tom Capelli at High Country Guide Service, 505/588-7674.

Navajo Lake

Navajo has a variety of species, both warm and cold water. It has the largest kokanee in New Mexico, most of which are concentrated in the main body of the lake, though some are found all the way up into Colorado on both arms of the lake.

The hot spot for kokanee on Navajo is around the mouth of Frances Canyon, not far from Sims Mesa Marina. For more information contact Sims Mesa Marina at 505/320-0885 or 320-0059 or the Navajo Lake State Park Headquarters at 505/632-2278.

NEW YORK

New York is one of only two Eastern states that has had any success with the kokanee. New York's kokanee are concentrated in a few small lakes and ponds in the Adirondacks, in the northeastern part of the state. New York is expanding its kokanee program, having introduced the fish into two new ponds in 1995.

All populations are made up of stockers; no one is aware of any successful natural reproduction of kokanee. Eggs come from Connecticut, which produces about 300,000 per year and keeps about half.

Favorite methods of fishing for kokes in New York include slow trolling with a Lake Clear Wabbler (see the chapter on trolling) used as a dodger, with a baited hook, fly, or small lure trailing the Wabbler by a foot to eighteen inches on a light mono leader. Joe Hackett, an Adirondack fishing guide who fishes a lot for kokanee, says he often finds the little rascals at 6 to 8 feet in the summer.

If you are headed up that way and want to fish for kokanee, get in touch with Joe Hackett and fish with him for a day or two before striking out on your own. He owns Tahawus Guide Service, is fully licensed and competent, and will show you a good time and lots of fish. His number is 518/523-4408.

OREGON

Billy Chinook

This central Oregon lake is located on three rivers, the Crooked, Deschutes, and Metolius. This is a fine lake for good numbers of medium sized kokanee.

Try the area around the confluence of the Deschutes/Crooked and Metolius arms and on down to the area of the dam. In the Metolius arm, search carefully with your finder around Chinook Island. Kokes sometimes lie just off the upstream shore of the island, or farther up near the bank on the Warm Springs Indian Reservation side. In late summer, search up the Metolius in the area of Monty Campground. For information call Oregon Fish and Wildlife (503)872-5268.

Paulina

Paulina (1530 acres) holds state records for kokanee (4.4 pounds) and brown trout (27 pounds 3/4 ounce). That it is productive is shown by Phil Johnson's experience there in the summer of 1995. Phil and a fellow fisherman took their limits 7 days in a row, trolling with Wee Tads.

Not far from Paulina is East Lake (1044 acres). It too is the home of large kokanee and huge brown trout. East is reputed to be hotter for kokanee this year (1996) than Paulina. Try trolling in the vicinity of the White Slide. Call Paulina Resort for information 503/536-2240.

The Kokanee Page on the Internet

By all means, if you are interested in Oregon Kokanee, check out the Kokanee Page on the Internet. Robert Nolan is performing a valuable service with this page.

If folks from around the country start to contribute, it will become all the more valuable. The address is: http://www.dnc.net/users.nolanr/kokanee.html

UTAH

Flaming Gorge

Nineteen ninety-six has been a good year for kokanee on the Gorge. Many fish over three pounds were taken. Biologists say that next year will be leaner, but 1998 promises to show a good crop.

Good information can be found from fisheries personnel at Dutch John 435/885-3164.

Strawberry/Soldier Creek

Originally two reservoirs, Strawberry and Soldier Creek were joined a few decades ago. The connecting arm is called the Narrows, and is a good fishery. Soldier Creek is reputed to be a tad better for kokanee, Strawberry for cutthroats. The koke fishery has suffered recently; call before you go.

The best summer kokanee spots I have found are near the Ladders at the northeast corner of the Strawberry side, between the island near Jake's Bay and the bank (the "island" is often covered), just out around the corner to the north of Strawberry Bay, near the forks inside the Narrows, and about 30 yards out from the northwest bank at the Soldier Creek end of the Narrows.

For food, bait, lures and equipment, advice, licenses, maps, excellent rental boats, and good friendly help, stop by the Strawberry Bay Marina and see Doug Phillips or one of his people. Doug's restaurant at Strawberry Bay Marina has some of the best hamburgers you ever threw a lip over. There are good rooms for rent here too.

Moon Lake

Moon Lake is an interesting lake situated in the Uintas 42 miles north of the town of Duchesne. The lake gets it name from its shape, somewhat like a crescent moon.

The Ute Indians were sorely frightened of Moon Lake. They had a legend of an ancient canoe race, during which the "Moon Lake Monster" came from the cold depths and swallowed up all the canoes. Older, more traditional Utes still do not go out on the lake.

There is a charming little resort at Moon Lake, named, appropriately, Moon Lake Resort. The resort has belonged to the family of Kathy Clark since 1962. It offers nice cabins with showers, toilets, and kitchens, horseback riding, outfitter and guide services, boat and mountain bike rentals, and a lodge with candy, pop, beer, some groceries, and games.

Moon lake is a nice place to go, kick back, stay awhile, forget the routine. It's a good place to catch several pink-fleshed little kokanee and grill them in the evening as the light dims and the cool air moves in, as the deer and elk come out into the meadows to munch the tender mountain grass.

Call Kathy and reserve a cabin and a boat. The number at the resort is 435/532-2900.

The author's son, Jim, demonstrates the proper form for trolling when kokanee are shallow and a downrigger is not needed.

This spawner, held by a pretty student from Springville, Utah Middle School, has been stripped of milt by Utah state biologists.

WASHINGTON

Washington has at least 79 kokanee waters, the populations of 33 of which are naturally self-sustaining. This state probably has more kokanee than anywhere else on the continent except British Columbia and Alaska.

Chelan

This is the largest natural lake in Washington. From the village of Stehekin at the upper end, a place reached only by boat, plane, or foot, to Chelan at the lower end is about 50 miles. The lake averages about a mile wide and goes as deep as 1500 feet. Though the lake offers several species, it is claimed that kokanee are the most popular.

A good place to begin gathering information would be Lake Chelan State Park at 509/687-3710.

Franklin D. Roosevelt Lake

FDR holds an astonishing 30-plus species of fish, including walleye, rainbow trout, yellow perch, whitefish, cutthroat trout, largemouth and smallmouth bass, various sunfishes, carp, pike, bullheads, giant white sturgeon, and some of the finest kokanee found anywhere.

It is uncommon in kokanee fishing to find fish over two pounds readily available, fish over four pounds not uncommon, and still have large numbers of fish ready and willing to strike your lures. When it is good here at Roosevelt, it can be that good. Kokanee of over six pounds have been electroshocked, according to Tim Peone, Manager of the Spokane Tribal Hatchery.

Some of the traditionally hotter areas for kokanee include Swawilla basin, Keller Ferry, Plum Point, the Goat Farm, the San Poil arm, and Whitestone.

Level fluctuations are probably to blame for the terrible kokanee fishing in FDR in 1996. There have even been rumors that a lot of kokanee were washed from the dam during the flushes designed to help the anadromous salmon. This seems less than far-fetched when one considers what happened at Dworshak, where the kokanee population dropped from 1.3 million in February 1996 to 150,000 in April, after similar flushing activity.

A good source of general fishing information for FDR and northeast Washington is Seven Bays Marina at 509/725-1676.

Loon Lake

Loon is easily accessible and offers a great variety of species, including rainbow, mackinaw, brook, smallmouth and largemouth bass, perch, crappie, pumpkinseed, bullhead, and kokanee. Kokanee are very popular in this lake.

Loon is situated about 30 miles north of Spokane on Highway 395. This would be an excellent area for a summer kokanee trip, as there are at least four lakes in the vicinity that hold kokanee.

Opening day in the spring of 1996 saw the largest kokanee anyone can remember for that time of year on Loon. Silvers of 18 inches were not uncommon.

Early to midsummer is typically trolling time, with lead line being popular. Downriggers work well too, however. As the summer progresses, one has to troll early in the morning to beat the speed demons with their ski boats and jet skis.

Once they get on the lake, the kokes seem to disappear.

From mid-July on, many folks stillfish at night. Mackinaw and rainbows are often taken in addition to kokanee. For information or equipment call Linda Haley at Granite Point Park 509/233-2100.

WYOMING

Flaming Gorge

Without a doubt the best kokanee lake in Wyoming at this time is Flaming Gorge, which Wyoming shares with Utah. In the summer of 1996, as I write this, good numbers of kokes in the three-pound range are coming from the Gorge. There are lots of two-pounders, with an occasional fish of four-pounds and over.

Next year's mature kokanee age class, now 2+ years old, is composed of fewer individuals, so fishing may be a tad less productive than this year. There will still be some fish from this year's group that will show up as 1997's big boys. 1998 looks good, as there is a strong group of 1+ fish in the lake.

Hattie

A huge kokanee was taken from Hattie in the summer of 1994 by Victor Chesna of Laramie. Not recognizing this fish as a kokanee, Victor butchered it and took it to a local butcher shop to have it smoked.

Before he gutted the fish and removed its head, Victor weighed it on his tackle box scales. That scale showed that the fish weighed 8.5 pounds. If Victor's scale was even close, the fish would have beaten the Wyoming state record by 3.5 pounds.

The attendant at the market weighed Victor's kokanee sans head and viscera, in which condition it weighed 5.57 pounds, still taking the Wyoming state record by over half a pound.

Victor's state record was beaten by a 5.58 pound kokanee taken in Flaming Gorge in the summer of 1995. Beating the Lake Hattie fish by a hundredth of a pound, the Flaming Gorge fish would have been at least 2.92 pounds short, had Chesna's fish been weighed whole. Wyoming fisheries biologists and managers, after examining the photo, feel Chesna's fish would have weighed in the 8.5 to 9.0 pound area. The world record kokanee, taken from Okanagan Lake, B.C. in 1988 by Norman Kuhn, weighed 9 pounds 6 ounces.

YUKON

If you are in or are going to the Yukon, call 867/667-5110 and ask Susan Thompson about the kokanee in the pothole lakes near Snag Junction and Ibex Valley. Both locations are near Whitehorse and are easily accessible. Susan has worked hard to get kokanee established in these lakes, and her efforts are paying off.

The four lakes in the Yukon that have native kokes, Kathleen, Louise, Sockeye, and Frederick, are hard to reach.

Section Six

APPENDIX

Appendix

STATE-BY-STATE TABLES OF KOKANEE LAKES

About the Tables

Much of this data will be outdated by the time you read it. However, perhaps the information given here will help you get started in researching the kokanee fishing prospects in areas that are of interest to you. I would advise you never to go fishing anywhere far away without spending some time on the phone before you start out. These statistics can change, not only from year to year or season to season, but from week to week.

I have tried to provide you with numbers you can call to get started in any area. Occasionally, the best I have been able to do was a general number for the state department of game and fish, but they will normally be able to direct you to sources of current information.

Key to Fish Species *(for all tables)*

A=Atlantic salmon
Al=Alewife
BH=Bullhead
Bk=Brook trout
Br=Brown trout
BT=Bull trout
Bu=Burbot
CC=Channel cat
CB=Cuttbow (CT/RT)
Ch=Chinook salmon
Co=Silver salmon
CP=Chain picker
CT=Cutthroat trout
Cr=Crappie
DV=Dolly Varden
F=Flathead cat
LB=Largemouth bass
LT=Lake trout
NP=Northern pike
P=Panfish, bluegill, etc.
PS=Anadromous Pacific salmon
S=Squawfish
Sal=Anadromous salmon (any species)
SB=Smallmouth bass
SE=Sockeye (anadromous)
SP=Splake (Bk/LT)
SS=Self-sustaining kokanee
T=Rainbow trout
TM=Tiger muskie
W=Whitefish
WE=Walleye
Y=Yellow/white perch

Alaska

Kokanee are certainly found in Alaska, particularly in the southeastern part of the state, on the Kenai Peninsula, and Kodiak Island. Doubtless there are hundreds of lakes in other parts of the state that also hold kokanee.

According to John Burke, Deputy Director of Alaska Department of Fish and Game's Sport Fish Division, kokanee are not taken too seriously in Alaska. More popular are the various species of anadromous salmon, cutthroat trout, Dolly Varden, Arctic char, and sheefish.

I have not included a table on this big and lovely state because, frankly, little is known about the kokanee in Alaska. When asked to name their best kokanee lakes, Alaska officials directed me toward the trophy cutthroat lakes in southeast Alaska and the Kenai Peninsula, stating that there were "far too many to list". There are kokanee up to 10 or 12 inches in some of these lakes.

I cannot imagine traveling to Alaska to fish for kokanee. There are too many giant kings, coho, Dolly Varden, and Arctic char to take up one's fishing hours. Then there are the halibut big enough to fill a pickup bed. How, in that environment, could you get overly excited about a 10-inch kokanee?

For more information contact, Alaska Sport Division, P.O. Box 25526, Juneau, AK 99802, 907/465-4180.

British Columbia

Just setting foot in this paradise excites me to the point that I nearly forget why I am there. I think not only of kokanee, but of giant salmon and halibut, of moose, grizzlies, and wolverines. I think of beautiful, seemingly endless forest and of lakes the size of oceans. If I sound envious of those who live there, it may be because I am somewhat envious of those who live there.

I find it surprising, given the fishing opportunities there, but the kokanee is quite popular in B.C. There is even a beer named after him. That is no small honor. Find me a Bass Beer, a Trout Beer, or a Walleye Beer in the United States. The B.C. fisheries people declare the kokanee the third most popular game fish in the province. Along Kootenay Lake are advertisements of many fishing guides. A large portion of those, and of guides all over the southern half of the province, advertise kokanee fishing. One sign boasts kokanee up to six pounds.

B.C. has far too many kokanee lakes for me to get them all on a table. I have tried to get the most well-known lakes, but there are hundreds that hold kokanee. If you plan to go to a certain area within B.C., I suggest you do some serious phone research with the fisheries folks in that area. The numbers are listed after the table.

BRITISH COLUMBIA

Name of Lake	Area in Acres	Avg. Size Adult Koke	Comments	Other Species	Information
Alice	3000		Victoria good also	T, CT, DV, Co	North Island 250/387-4573
Great Central	12560			T, CT, S	Central V.C. 250/387-4573
Cowichan	15300			T, CT, Br, DV, Sal	South V.C.I. 250/387-4573
Mohun	1544			DV, CT, T	Pt. Hardy 250/387-4573
Lois Horsehoe Nanton Dodd	3490 700 300 1067		Four good lakes close together	CT, T	Powell River Surrey 604/582-5222
Alouette	2600			CT, DV, LT	Maple Ridge Surrey 604/582-5222
Kawkawa	145			T, CT	Hope Surrey 604/582-5222
Nicola	15351			Bu, T, W	Merrit Kamloops 250/371-6200
Douglas	1606			Bu, T	Merrit Kamloops 250/371-6200
Wood	2322	1-5 lbs.		T, W	Kelowna 250/490-8200
Kalamika	8645			T, W	Vernon Kamloops 250/371-6200
Okanagan[WR]	864500	10"		W, T	Vernon Kamloops 250/371-6200
Osoyoos	9880			LB, Y, W, T	Osoyoos 250/490-8200
Arrow	66700		Good numbers	T, DV	Nakusp 250/489-8540
Kootenay	100000		Good numbers	T, DV, W, LT, Bu	Creston, Nelson 250/354-6333
Koocanusa	100 miles long	To 2 lbs. avg. 12"	Full July through November	CT, W, DV, Bu, T	Cranbrook 250/489-8540

[WR] The all-tackle world record kokanee salmon, 9 pounds 6 ounces, was caught in Okanagan Lake in June 1988. Some biologists list the future of kokanee in Okanagan as "not good" due in part to the presence of *Mysis relicta.*

Name of Lake	Area in Acres	Avg. Size Adult Koke	Comments	Other Species	Information
Kinbasket			Wind, floating debris. Good numbers	T: 4 lbs.; DV, W, Br	New Denver 250/354-6333
Slocan	28 miles long	1 lb.	Good numbers	T to 11 lbs. DV to 15 lbs.	New Denver 250/354-6333
Lac la Hache		2 lb.	Parallels Hwy. 97	T, LT	Lac la Hache 100 Mile Hse.; Williams Lake 250/398-4530
Horse			Rb to 4 lbs.	LT, Bu, T	100 Mile Hse.; Williams Lake 250/398-4530
Bridge	8645			T, LT, Bu	100 Mile Hse.; Williams Lake 250/398-4530
Eagan	297	1 lb.		T	100 Mile Hse.; Williams Lake 250/398-4530
McLeese		2 lbs.	Troll w/ worm. Flatfish	T	Williams Lake 250/398-4530
Puntzi		2 lbs.		T	Tatla Lake 250/565-6135
Williston	Largest lake in B.C.		Dangerous storms, big water Ocean-worthy boats only	DV T, W,	MacKenzie Ft. St. John 250/787-3295

B.C. Fisheries Offices

Main Office, 2-780 Blanshard St., Victoria, British Columbia, Canada, V8V 1X4. 250/387-4573.

Region 8, 3547 Skahe Lake Rd., Suite 201, Penticton, British Columbia, Canada, V2A 7K2, 250/490-8200.

Region 7, 10033-110th Ave., Rm. 200, Fort St. John, BC, Canada, V1J 6M7, 250/787-3295.

Region 7, Plaza 400, 1011-4th Ave., 3rd Floor, Prince George, BC V2L 3H9, 250/565-6135.

Region 6, 3726 Alfred St., Bag 5000, Smithers, BC, V0J 2N0, 250/847-7303.

Region 5, 540 Borland St., Williams Lake, BC, Canada, V2G 1R8. 250/398-4530.

Region 4, 333 Victoria St., Suite 401, Nelson, BC, Canada, V1L 4K3, 250/354-6333.

Region 4, 205 Industrial Rd. G, Cranbrook, BC, Canada, V1C 6H3. 250/489-8540.

Region 3, 1259 Dalhousie Dr., Kamloops, BC, Canada, V2C 5Z5. 250/371-6200.

Region 2, 10334-152 A St., Surrey, BC, Canada, V3R 7P8. 604/582-5222.

Region 1, 2569 Kenworth Rd., Nanaimo, BC, Canada, V9T 4P7. 250/751-3100.

CALIFORNIA

Name of Lake	Area/ Acres	Avg. Size Adult Koke	1995 Plant/1996 Planned (X1000)	Other Species	Information
Bass	1200	12-14"	50/50	T, LB, SB, P, CC	916/653-7664
Boca	1000	16-19"	0/30	SS, P, CC, Bk, T, Br	916/653-7664
Bowman	800	12"	0/100		
Bucks	1820	10-12"	0/0	SS, LT, P, Bk, CC, **T,** Br	916/653-7664
Bullard's Bar	4600	10-12"	325/300	**T, LB**, Br, P, C, SB	916/653-7664
Commanche	7700	12"	150	T, LB, P, CC	209/763-5178
Don Pedro Best koke lakes	13000.	18-21"	0/0	**T**, LB, SB, Bk, Br, CC, P, SS	209/852-2396
Donner	1440	12"	200/150	**LT, Br**, T	530/587-4844
Echo	300	12"	0/0	SS, T, CT, Br	916/653-7664
Fallen Leaf	1445	14-16"	102/75	T, Br	916/653-7664
Folsom	11930	12-13"	160/250	**T, LB,** SB, C, P, **CH**	916/653-7664
Hell Hole	1300. Bad road	14-18"	70/100	Br, T	916/653-7664
Huntington	1262	14"	40/50	**RT, Br**	209/893-6750
Little Grass Valley	1600	14-16"	0/40	**Br, RT**, SS	916/675-2462
Pardee	2250	12-15"	150/100	**T**, Br, LB, SB, P, **CC**	209/772-1472
Shaver	2000	14-16"	50/50	T, LT, LB, P, SB, Br, Bk, CC	916/653-7664
Stampede	3440	13"	300/150	T, Br, LT	916/653-7664
Tahoe	121600 Depth: 1645 ft.	16-24"	300/200	**LT,** Br, T, CT	916/581-6900
Trinity	17000	10-12"	0/0	**T, SB,** LB, P, CC	800/487-4648
Union Valley	1600	12-18"	50/100	T	530/644-6048
Scotts Flat		12"	0/0	T, Br	916/653-7664
Lewiston		10-12"	0/0	T, **Br**, Bk	916/653-7664
Upper/Lower Twin Lakes	About 900 ea	9-12"	0/0	**Br,** T, SS	530/644-6048
Whiskeytown*	3220	13-17"	0/0	SS, T, LB, CC, **P**, Br	530/241-6584

Species shown in **bold** are abundant in that water.
* Self-sustaining population of kokanee.

COLORADO

Name of Lake	Area/ Acres	Comments	Avg. Size Adult Koke	Other Species	Information
Green Mt.	2125	Good koke lake	14"	LT, Sp	Kremmling
Turquoise	1500			T, CT, Br, Bk, LT	Leadville
Eleven Mile	3400	Big fish	16-24"	T, Br, NP	719/748-3401
Granby	7300	*Mysis* present. Kokes in decline	13-14"	LT, Br, T, CT, Sp	303/297-1192
Williams Fork	1810	Good koke lake near Green Mountain	17"	T, Br, LT, NP	Kremmling
Dillon	3200	Kokes no longer stocked		T, Br, Bk, Sp	Dillon
Ruedi	1000			T, Br, LT, Sp	Meredith
Blue Mesa	9000	Best koke lake in CO	15-16"	Br, T, Bk, LT	Gunnison
Beaver Creek	115			Br, T, Bk	South Fork
Ridgeway	1028	Promising		T, Br	Ridgeway
Vallecito	2700	Reliable Egg source	14"	RT, **Br,** CT, **NP**, WE	Bayfield
Williams Creek	340		12"	T, **Bk**	Pagosa Springs
Platoro	700	One of the highest reservoirs in the U.S.		T, Br	Del Norte
McPhee	4470	Promising	14-15"	T, Y, Cr, **CC**, P, LB, **SB**, WE	Dolores, Cortez
Gunnison River	26 miles		16"	T, Br, CT	Gunnison

A species entered in **bold** is abundant in that water.

CONNECTICUT

Name of Lake	Area/ Acres	Avg. Size Adult Koke	Comments	Other Species	Information
Wonoskopomuc or Lakeville	353	12"	Good	RT, CP, VP	Salisbury 806/424-3011
West Hill Pond	239	12"	Good	RT, SB	Barkhamsted 806/424-3011
East Twin	562	14"	Gone. No longer stocked	LB, YP, RT P, BH, CP	Salisbury 806/424-3011

GLACIER NATIONAL PARK

Name of Lake	Area/ Acres	Other Species	Boat Ramp	Road Access?
Bowman		CT, BT	Yes	Yes
Harrison		CT, BT	No	No
Josephine		Bk	No	No*
Kintla		CT, LT, BT	Yes	Yes
Lake McDonald**		LT, CT	Yes	Yes
Swiftcurrent	100	Bk	Yes***	Yes

* It is only about a mile hike to Josephine from Many Glacier Hotel. The fish are small.

**Lake McDonald is scenic, accessible, and crystal clear. Unfortunately, fishing is poor.

***Located next to Many Glacier Hotel, this lake has row boats available for rent.

Glacier Park Lodge 406/226/7800

IDAHO

Name of Lake	Area in Acres	Avg. Size Adult Koke	Comments	Other Species	Information
Spirit Lake	1300	7"	Small kokes, but plentiful	LT, T, Y, P	S.L. Taxidermy 208/623-5656
Pend Oreille	94600 1172" deep	10"	Medium kokes, Girard RT, good WF	LT, T W, CT, Y	Sand Point 208/334-3700
Coeur D' Alene	25100	10"	Medium kokes, king salmon	**T**, CT, NP, CC, Y	Fins & Feathers 208/667-9304
Priest Lake*	23700		Priest holds state record, but kokes are gone. Only LT now	LT, BT	Nordman 208/769-1414
Dworshak Reservoir	16000	17"		Bu, T, CT	Orofino 208/476-5418
Little Payette Lake	300	12"		T, W	McCall 208/334-3700
Deadwood Reservoir	3000			BT, CC, T, CT, W	Cascade 208/334-3700
Cascade Reservoir	30000	11		BT, Co, T, W, Bu, Y	Cascade 208/334-3700
Anderson Ranch Reservoir	5000	12		CC, T, Bu	208/334-3700
Redfish Lake	1500	13		BT, T, SE	208/334-3700

A species entered in **bold** is important in that water.
* State record kokanee, 6 pounds 9.5 ounces, 24.5 inches, Priest Lake, 1975. Caught by Jerry Verge.

MONTANA

Name of Lake	Area in Acres	Avg. Size Adult Koke	Comments	Other Species	Information or Nearby Town
Kootenai River		11"		W, T, BT	Troy
Spar	400	16"		CT, LT, Bk	Troy
Tobacco River			Off Koocanusa	T, BT	Eureka
Dickey	600	12"	Good fishing	Br, NP	Libby
Lake Koocanusa	46500	11"		WF, CT, RT, Bu, BT	Libby, Eureka
Crystal	178	14"	Dirt ramp, good koke	Y, T, LB	406/444-2535
Glen Lake	340	11"	YP over-populated. Poor fishing	W, T, Y	Libby
Bull	1250	14"	Ramp, camping	T, LB	Troy
Middle Thompson Lake	600	16-22"	Low catchrate	Y, T, LB	Libby
Ashley Lake*	3200	8-10"	Rough road, poor ramp	CB, Y	406/444-2535
Lake Alva	300			W, CT, BT, Y	Seeley Lake
Lake Inez	300			W, CT, BT, Y	Seeley Lake
Flathead	126117		No kokes	LT, W, T, CT, BT, Y, Bu	Polson,Kalispell, Bigfork
Mary Ronan	1490	11-12"	Popular	CT, T, LB, Y	Kalispell
Tally	1300		USFS campground and ramp	CT, Bu, NP	Kalispell
Blaine	370	10"	Limited access	T, BT, NP, LB, Y, Bu	Kalispell
Little Bitterroot	2900	11"	Great koke fishing, dirt ramp	T, Y	Kalispell
Salmon Lake	600			W, CT, Br, T, BT, Bu, Y	Seeley Lake
Seeley Lake	1300			W, CT, T, BT, LT, **Y**	Seeley Lake
Swan Lake	2700	11"	Two size classes	CT, T, BT, NP, W	Swan Lake
Georgetown	3000			Bk, T	Anaconda
Canyon Ferry	35300			T, Br, W, Y, Bu	Helena
Hauser Lake	3700	17"		T	Helena
Helena Valley	500			Y	Helena
Placid Lake	1100			W, CT, T BT, LB, Y	Missoula

continued on page 146...

MONTANA *continued...*

Name of Lake	Area in Acres	Avg. Size Adult Koke	Comments	Other Species	Information or Nearby Town
Holland	400	9"	Poor	CT	Missoula
Holter Lake	5000	17"		B, T, WE Y	Wolf Creek
Silver	400			BT, LT, T CT	Deer Lodge
Pishkun				T, NP, Y	Choteau
Deadman's Basin Reservoir	1900			Br, T, Co	Harlowton

A species entered in **bold** is abundant in that water.
* Ashley produced the world record hybrid cutthroat/rainbow ("cuttbow") trout in May 1982; 30 pounds 4 ounces, 35.75 inches long.

NEW MEXICO

Name of Lake	Area in Acres	Comments	Avg. Size Adult Koke	Other Species	Landmark or Nearby Town
Abiquiu Lake	4000	Kokanee secondary here	13"	CC, Cr, L B, SB, WE	Espanola
Eagle Nest	2000	Good numbers	14"	CT, T, Suckers	Eagle Nest
El Vado	3500	Future egg source	14"	Br, T	Chama
Heron	6000	State's egg source	17"	Br, T, LT	Chama
Navajo**	15000	Good numbers. Large size	17"	Br, T, LB, SB, CC, BT, Cr, BH	Aztec

** State record kokanee.

NEW YORK

Name of Lake or Pond	Area in Acres	Avg. Size Adult Koke	Comments	Other Species	Information, County
Kushegua Lake	375	12"	First stocking 1995	LT, BH, NP, Br	Franklin
Glass Lake		12"			Rensselaer
Clear Pond	87	11"	First stocking 1995	SP, BH, NP	Franklin
Long Pond	333	16"	Good access	LT, LB, SB	Franklin
Lower Mitchell Pond	24	12"		Br	Hamilton
Polliwog Pond	208	12"	Easy access	Br, Y, BH	Franklin
Colby			No ramp	Br, T	Franklin

* New York state record kokanee taken from Crane Pond, 17 inches, 1 pound 13 ounces.

OREGON

Name of Lake	Area/ Acres	Comments	Avg. Size Adult Koke	Other Species	Information County, Town
Lake Billy Chinook	3915	Lots of kokes most years	11"	SB, LB, **BT**, Br, T,	Jefferson, Madras
Blue Lake	54	Few and small. Beautiful lake	9"	T	Jefferson, Bend
Crane Prairie Reservoir	4167	One of best in Oregon. Rich in nutrients, shallow	13"	LB, T Bk	Deschutes, Bend
Crescent Lake	4547	Big kokes, but few	15"	LT, W, Br, T	Klamath, Oakridge
Detroit Lake	3580	Kokes go deep (100') in late summer	14"	Bk, CC, BH	Marion/Detroit, Salem
East Lake**	1044	Big kokes in 1996	15"	T, **Br**, A, Co	Deschutes,Bend
Elk Lake	405	Ask about the Kokanee Hole. Small and abundant	7-9"	Bk	Deschutes, Bend
Elk Lake (#2)	64	Hwy. 22 from Detroit. Poor road. No ramp	8"	T, Bk, CC	Marion, Detroit
Fourmile	760	Large self-sustaining population	6-10"	T, Bk	Klamath, Klamath Falls
Green Peter	3700	Kokanee are very popular	11"	T, LB	Linn, Sweet Home
Haystack	250	Level changes. Good for nice kokes	16"	**P**, LB, SB, BH, T, Br, Cr	Jefferson, Madras 8 miles S.
Lake of the Woods	1146	Catch rate not high	11"	LT, BH, T, Bk	Klamath, Klamath Falls
Miller Lake	550	Kokes over-abundant. Good browns	8"	RT, Br	Klamath, Crater Lake National Park
O'Dell Lake	3582	Tons of small kokes. Big lakers	10"	T, BT, DV, LT	Klamath, Klamath Lake
Paulina Lake	1530	State records Koke: 4.4lbs.,1989 Brown: 27 lbs. 3/4oz. 1993	15"	T, **Br**	Deschutes Bend 541/536-2240
Simtustus Lake	540	Need permit from CTWS from Warm Springs grocery. Fair angling	10"	LB, T, Br, BT	Jefferson, Madras. Near Lake Billy Chinook.
Suttle Lake	250	Big numbers, small kokes. Large (18") some years	9"	T, **Br**	Jefferson, Bend
Timothy Lake	1290	Tons of crayfish	11"	T, **Bk**, CT	Clackamas, Near Portland

continued on page 148....

OREGON *continued...*

Name of Lake	Area/ Acres	Comments	Avg. Size Adult Koke	Other Species	Information County, Town
Triangle	280	Early and late to beat skiers	10"	LB, P, CC, Y, CT	Lane, Junction City
Waldo Lake	6300	Very clear. Dangerous wind. Mosquitoes	10"	Bk	Lane, Eugene
Wallowa Lake	1500	Kokanee may be eating *Mysis*	9"	**T**, LT, DV	Joseph
Wickiup Reservoir	10300	Changing conditions and levels make fishing hard.	16"	**Br**, Co, T, W	Deschutes, LaPine, Bend

Species showing in **bold** are abundant in that lake.
For more information on these lakes, and others with kokanee, call Oregon Department of Fish and Wildlife, Portland 503/872-5268.

UTAH

Name of Lake	Area/ Acres	Comments	Avg. Size Adult Koke	Other Species	Information
Flaming Gorge*	42000	Very good	14-19"	LT, Br, CR, T	Dutch John
Strawberry*	17,000	Big kokes, but difficult	15-24"	T, CT	Heber
Porcupine[n]	200	Very good	16-18"	T, Br, CT, W,	Logan
Moon*	7 mile long	Good at north end for small kokes	9-10"	T, Br, CT, Grayling	Duchesne, Moon Lake Resort
Stateline	200	Small kokes	10-12"	Br, CT, T, W, Sp	801/476-2740
Causey	300	Good. No ramp	17-19"	T, CT, Bk, W	801/476-2740
East Canyon	250	Kokes gone; water quality down due to grazing and development at Park City		T	801/476-2740

* Kokanee at least partially self sustaining.
[n] Porcupine has all natural reproduction of kokanee.

WASHINGTON STATE

Name of Lake	Area/ Acres	Comments	Avg. Size Adult Koke	Other Species	Information or County
Alder[w]	2931			T, CT, LB, Y, BH	Pierce
American	1125	Koke fair, few big T	16"	T, Y, BH CT, Rock Bass	Pierce
Baker[w]	3616	May/June, fall good numbers		T, DV, CT	Whatcom County
Banks	24900			WE, T, W, Y, P	Grant
Bead[w]	720	April, May no boat access		LT, BU	Pend Oreille
Billy Clapp/ Long Lake[w]	1010			T, CT, Y, P, BH	Grant
Bonaparte	160	USFS camping, resort		T, LT, Bk	509/486-2828
Bumping[w]	1310	Best in May for 6-9" fish	8-11"	T	Yakima
Cascade	171	Fair	9"	T, CT	San Juan, Orcas Island, Moran State Park
Cavanaugh[w]	844	Some trophy CT		T, CT, Bk, LB	Skagit
Chapman	146	"good catches, generous limits"		LB, SB, RT	Spokane
Chelan[w]	33104	April through June	16-18"	T, CT, LT, SB, DV, Bu, CC	Chelan State Park 509/687-3710
Clear Lake	155	Good fishing	12"	T	509/299-3830
Cle Elum	4810	Generous koke catch limit	8-14"	LT, Bu, BT, W, Br, DV	7.3 miles NE of town of Cle Elum
Conconully		Early morning	12-16"	T	509/826-4148
Cooper[w]	120	No outboard motors	8"	Bk, T	Near upper Cle Elum River
Crescent	5127	Natural reproduction		T, SS	Olympic National Park
Cushman	4000			CT, BT (closed for BT)	Mason
Davis	146	"good early and late"		LB, T, Bk	Pend Oreille
Deep[w]	104	"fair"	11"	T, Lt	Grant County
Deep	39	Kokes are native	10"	T, CT, Y, Cr, BH	King County
Deer[w]	1163	Fair numbers	17-19"	LB, SB, Y, T, LT, Br, P, CC	360/902-2200
Devereaux	94	Fall		T	Mason

continued on page 150...

WASHINGTON *continued...*

Name of Lake	Area/ Acres	Comments	Avg. Size Adult Koke	Other Species	Information or County
Horseshoe[w]	128	generous limit, chumming		Cr, LB, Y, P, CC	Pend Oreille
Kachess[w]	4540	Start early June	8-10"	T, CT, Bu, DV, LT	Near Interstate 90, Exit 62
Keechelus[w]	2560	Start early June	10-12"	Bu	Exit 62
Loon[w]	1120	Huge in early summer 1996	17-19"	B, SB, BH, P, T, Br, Bk, LT	Stevens Granite Point Park, 509/233-2100
Lost[w]	10	July-Aug.	8"	Bk, CT	Kittitas County
Lost	122		9"	T	Mason County
Mason	977	Good numbers		RB, Sea-run CT, T	Mason County
Merwin[w]	4810	Fish for kokes from bank at Merwin Park	18"	Co	Clark
Morton	66	Koke not major species		T	King
Mountain	198	June & Sept.		CT, Bk	See Cascade
Osoyoos[w]	5723 (2036 in WA)	Koke natural reproduction		T, LB, SB, P, SS	Okanogan
Padden	152	Some big RT		T	Whatcom
Palmer	2063	Year-round water. Good SB		SB, P, Bu	Okanogan
Pierre[w]	106	Fair numbers		BH, LB, Br, T	See Deer
Pleasant[w]	500	8 to 20" limit	17-21"	CT	Clallam County
Rimrock[w]	2530	Very good May/July	8-13"	T	Yakima
Roesiger	352			T, LB, P, BH, Y	Snohomish
Roosevelt[w]	79000 to 81389	Among best in U.S.A	15-25"	T, Br, WE, BU, W, Y	Seven Bays Marina, 509/725-1676
Rufus Wood[w]					
Samish	814	Kokes start May	13-15"	LB, Cr, T, CT	Whatcom
Sammamish	4897	One of best SB lakes in WA		LB, SB, YP, CT, CC	309/402-2200
Sawyer	279	Fair kokes, good CT		T, CT, Y, P, LB, SB, BH	Same as above
Shannon[w]	2148	Rough access		Co	Skagit
Silver	102	Too many YP		T, CT, Y	Snohomish
St. Clair	270			T, LB, Y, P, Cr	Thurston
Stevens	1021	May-Aug. Access for disabled	16-18"	T, LB, Y, BH, CT, SB	Snohomish

continued on page 151...

WASHINGTON *continued...*

Name of Lake	Area/ Acres	Comments	Avg. Size Adult Koke	Other Species	Information or County
Summit	530	Good koke lake	9-12"	T, CT, LB, Y, BH	Thurston
Sutherland[w]	361	"Good to excellent"	12"	CT to 5 lbs., T	12 miles W of Port Angeles
Tapps	2296	Fair May-August		LB, SB, T	Pierce
Toad	29	"Some kokanee"		T	Whatcom
Washington[w]	22138	Starts May		T, CT, LB, CC SB, P, Y, Sal	King
Ward	67		10"	T, LB	Thurston
Whatcom	5003	Few big CT. Good SB North end. Egg source	6-9"	CT, LB, SB, Y	Whatcom
Wilderness	67			T	King
Yale[w]	3802	Excellent koke lake	13"	CT, DV	20 miles E of Woodland

Species shown in **bold** are abundant in that water.
[w] Kokanee at least partially self-sustaining in these waters.

WYOMING

Name of Lake	Area/ Acres	Avg. Size Adult Koke	Comments	Other Species	Information or Nearby Town
Fremont	4996	18"		LT, T, Br	307/777-4600
Middle Piney	120		Stocked 1995	T, CT	307/777-4600
Boulder	1400	16"		LT	307/367-4352
New Fork, Upper	700	12"		LT	307/777-4600
New Fork, Lower	370	12"		Bk, LT	307/777-4600
Fontenelle	7000	18"	Kokanee population small, but growing	CT, BR, BT, T, W, Su, Ch	307/875-3223
Flaming Gorge*	42000	20"	Two strains of kokanee	B, Br, CT, **LT**, T, CC,W	307/875-3223
Hattie	6500	18"	Irrigation storage reservoir. No kokanee spawning	Br, LT, T, Y	307/777-4600
Green River			No resident population. Spawning stream only	CT, CC	307/875-3223

*State record
Species in **bold** abundant in that water.

YUKON TERRITORY

According to Fisheries Technician Supervisor Susan Thompson, there are four lakes in the Yukon that hold native kokanee. In an effort to make this species more available to more anglers, Susan and others have been taking eggs from the lakes with native kokanee—most of these lakes are relatively inaccessible. They have been incubating them and raising fry in a private hatchery in Whitehorse, and stocking them in two pothole lakes near Whitehorse.

Susan is a delightful young woman; if you are lucky when you call, you will get an opportunity to talk with her. She is basically the kokanee program in the Yukon. Should you be heading up that way, she can tell you what you need to know to catch a koke up there in the Great White North.

YUKON

Name of Lake	Area/ Acres	Avg. Size Adult Koke	Comments	Other Species	Location Town, Phone
Kathleen		14-16"	Limit 2. Barbless hooks. Natives		Kluane National Park, 867/634-7250
Louise		14-16"	Limit 2. Barbless hooks. Natives		Kluane National Park, 867/634-7250
Sockeye		14-16"	Natives		Kluane National Park, 867/634-7250
Frederick		10-12"	Natives		867/667-5110
A pothole lake near Snag Junction		Time will tell	Stocked		NW of Whitehorse, 867/667-5110
Pothole Lake in Ibex Valley		We'll see	Stocked		Just outside Whitehorse, 867/667-5110

COOKIN' KOKANEE

The following are a few of the many good ways to prepare kokanee. If you want to experiment, most any recipe suitable for oily fish (salmon, trout, tuna...) works well for kokanee. Kokes are among the most flavorful of freshwater fish. They do not lend themselves to frying and deep frying as well as some other fish, however. Try barbecuing, baking, broiling, smoking, and canning.

BARBECUING

It was Heron Lake guide Tom Capelli who first showed us the wisdom in barbecuing kokanee. He has a grill on his pontoon boat and frequently serves up big plates of steaming barbecued kokanee and ranch style beans for his clients. Such a meal, eaten out in the clear air, made of fish fresh from cold Heron Lake waters, is not soon forgotten. The advice on care and cleaning, presented elsewhere, applies to any kokanee or to any fish you catch and intend to eat.

The process starts with catching a kokanee. When you accomplish that, put it in the cooler on crushed ice and let it stay cold, as it was when it came up from the deep. That makes all the difference in taste.

Clean your fish by removing its head and viscera and washing it thoroughly in cold lake water. Be sure to remove the kidney; it looks like a long, slender blood clot settled just inside the backbone in the body cavity. Don't bother removing skin or scales.

Salt and pepper each cleaned fish and wrap it in aluminum foil. Wrap fish in the foil singly, or not more than two per foil pack. Place the wrapped fish on the grill. Allow them to cook for about 10 minutes. If the fire is of the correct intensity, the fish will be sizzling and cooking audibly by that time. Open the foil and check them.

The skin should be easily separated from the cooked side. Remove and discard that skin and allow the fish to continue cooking on the other side with foil only loosely closed.

Soon you can roll the fish over and remove the skin from the other side. As the flesh cooks, it turns from the nearly translucent orange/pink to an opaque pinkish white. When it comes easily off the bone and the meat near the bone looks opaque, it is ready to serve. It will probably need more salt and pepper.

Serve a whole fish or a part of it on a paper plate with a generous helping of ranch style beans (see Appendix C) that have been heated over the fire in the open can.

I challenge anyone not to make a "hawg" of themselves on such fare. Don't start this cooking process until you have accumulated an ample supply of fish. More than one proud boat captain turned chef has been thrown overboard when hungry guests discovered that there were no more kokanee.

BROILING

Beth's Broiled Kokanee

We found this to be a real kokanee treat. The version with green chilies and onions is our all-time favorite way of preparing kokanee in the oven.

Cover inside of broiling pan with aluminum foil. Spray surface with no stick cooking spray. Place cleaned fish, thoroughly rinsed and dried, (whole, skin on, sans heads) on tray.

Inside each body cavity, lightly salt and add a mixture of 2 tablespoons canned chopped green chilies and 2 tablespoons diced fresh onion. Broil fish for a few minutes. When skin has browned and blistered, turn fish over and do the same to other side. Then remove blistered skin from one side and discard. Lightly butter and season flesh with salt, lemon pepper, and a touch of garlic salt. Let broil for a few more minutes until done (flakes easily from bone). Turn fish over and remove remaining skin, butter and season flesh and broil until done.

Variation: do not use chilies and onions in body cavity. Lightly salt body cavity. After removal of browned and blistered skin, season flesh with butter and salt. When ready to eat, use squeezed lemon juice on flesh and season to taste.

SMOKING

Tom Capelli's "High Country" Smoked Kokanee

Smoker Brine

6 cups water (room temperature)
3/4 cup salt
1/2 cup brown sugar
2 tsp. garlic powder
1/2 tsp. dill

1. Mix all ingredients into water
2. Soak fish (preferably skinned) in solution for 3 hours.
3. Remove fish and place on paper towel-lined baking dish.
   Place in refrigerator overnight.
4. Place fish in smoker and smoke for two hours or until done.
5. Remove from smoker and gorge until a doctor is needed.

CANNING

Tom Capelli's Canned Heron Lake Salmon and Trout

Salmon or trout *(approximately two 12-inch fish per pint)*
Pint canning jars
Canning salt
Cider vinegar
Jalapeno peppers (optional)

1. Skin and clean fish on the lake. Ice down fish immediately to preserve fresh flavor.
2. Cut fish to "jar" length, saving smaller pieces for filler. Soak cut fish for 30 minutes in water to which has been added 1 teaspoon of canning salt per fish.
3. Wash pint jars and lids in hot soapy water and rinse with hot water.
4. Fill jars with water and place open in canner.
   Fill pressure canner to top ring of jars with water and 2/3 cup vinegar (to prevent water stains in canner rack and on jars). Heat water to boiling. Scald jars in the boiling water in the canner (for sterilization).
5. Remove jars from canner one at a time. Empty water from each jar back into canner. Fill jar with fish to top ring. Pack fish tightly, filling voids with smaller pieces. Insure that all air pockets are removed.
6. Add 1/4 tsp. canning salt and 1/2 tablespoon cider vinegar to each jar. (For a Southwestern flavor, add one whole fresh jalapeno, with stem removed, to each jar.*)
7. Clean jar edges with clean, damp cloth. Put on lids, hand tighten (not too tight).
8. Place jars on rack in pressure canner. Hot water level should be to 3/4 height of jars. Close pressure canner lid.
9. Turn heat on high. Start counting time when pressure regulator starts "jiggling" (0 pressure in canning terms). Reduce heat, but maintain jiggling.
10. Cook for 90 minutes at zero pressure. Remove canner from hot burner immediately.
11. Let pressure canner cool normally approximately 30-60 minutes. (Touching the weight on the pressure vent should cause no pressure release.) Remove jars with jar tongs and set on towel to cool. The further cooling aids in the sealing process of jars. Check seal; determine that there is no leakage (lid surface concave and tight, no give when pressed with thumb or tapped with a metal object). Refrigerate or immediately use any jars that did not seal.
12. Clean and lubricate pressure canner seal with cooking oil.
13. Wipe off jars and tighten lids next day. Store jars.

** For a little less heat and a unique flavor, substitute a mild green chili for the jalapeno.*

Tom Capelli's Pickled Salmon/Trout

3 lbs. fish fillets cut into bite size pieces
3/4 cup canning salt
distilled vinegar (enough to cover fish)
5-6 onions, sliced

Put fish pieces and salt in a crock jar, cover with vinegar, let stand for 7 days. Remove and put into container of fresh water and leave for 8 hours, remove and rinse in fresh water.

Pickling Solution

3/4 cup brown sugar
3/4 cup white wine
4 tsp. pickling spices tied in cheese cloth
1 cup water, 1 3/4 cup distilled vinegar
1 tsp. unflavored gelatin mixed in a small amount of water

Simmer brown sugar, white wine and pickling spices in water for 30 minutes. Cool and remove spices. Add vinegar and gelatin and stir well.

Layer onion slices and fish in quart jars. Pour pickling solution into jars. Distribute solution evenly among jars. Cover fish by adding more vinegar if needed. Allow fish to sit 48 hours turning jars occasionally. If fish is too sour, add white sugar to taste. Store in refrigerator.

GUIDES, EQUIPMENT, AND INFORMATION

GUIDES

Vance's Guide & Tackle, Vance Staplin, owner, P.O. Box 4045, Citrus Heights, CA 95611-4045.

High Country Guide Service, Tom Capelli, owner, HCR Box 1197, Rutheron, NM 87551, 505/588-7674

Dave's Guide Service, Cliff Dare, Manager, 695 Milnor Lake Rd., Troy, MT, 59935, 406/295-4487.

Tahawus Guide Service, Joseph Patrick Hackett, owner, Box 424, Lake Placid, NY 12946, 518/523-4408

McPhee Marina, P.O. Box 236, Lewis, CO 81327, 800/882-2038, 970/882-2257. Guides available for McPhee Reservoir.

Randi Wiig, Elk Creek Guide Services, 970/641-0707. Blue Mesa Reservoir.

Cliff Redmon, The Good Life Guide Service, Box 173, Lyman, WY 82937. 307/786-2132.

There are many more guide services. Contact the fisheries people of the state in which you arc interested.

EQUIPMENT

Fish Finders

LCD

Bottom Line, a division of Computrol, 499 E. Corporate Dr., Meridian, ID 83642. (208) 887-1000.

Eagle Electronics, P.O. Box 669, Catoosa, OK 74015, 800/324-1354.

Humminbird, a division of Texonic Industries Inc., 5 Humminbird Lane, Eufaula, AL 36027, 334/687-6613.

Fish Finders

Flashers

Vexilar, 200 W. 88th Street, Minneapolis, MN 55420, 612/884-5291.

Temperature/Depth Indicators

Vexilar, 200 West 88th St. Minneapolis, MN 55420, 612/884-5291. "Depththerm."

Bead Tackle, 600 Main St., Monroe, CT 06468.

Nu-Temp, Pal Products, Wisconsin Rapids, WI 54495, the Un-Reel.

Trolling Speed Indicators

Cabela's Trolling Speedometer, electric, to 5 mph, $69.99, 800/237-4444.

Luhr-Jensen, P.O. Box 297, Hood River, OR 97031, 503/386-3811.

Downriggers

Cannon, a division of Computrol, 499 E. Corporate Dr., Meridian, ID 83642. 208/887-1000.

Big Jon, 14393 Peninsula Dr., Traverse City, Michigan 49684. 616/223-4286.

Downrigger Releases

Sep's Sure Release, sold by Sep's Pro Fishing, Inc., P.O. Box 5356, Vacaville, CA 95696-5356. 707/449-8413, FAX 707/446-3122. Also Sep's Sure Stacker.

Vance's Release, sold by Vance's Guide & Tackle, Vance Staplin, owner, P.O. Box 4045, Citrus Heights, CA 95611-4045, 916/725-2383. Also Vance's Stacker.

Shasta Ultra Release, Shasta Tackle, P.O. Box 488, Bella Vista, CA 96008, 916/275-2278.

Divers

Big Jon, 14393 Peninsula Dr., Traverse City, Michigan 49684. 616/223-4286.

Doelcher Products, 2970-A Bay Vista Ct., Benicia, CA 94510. 707/745-3488.

Luhr-Jensen, P.O. Box 297, Hood River, OR 97031. 503/386-3811.

Planing Boards, Side Planers

Luhr-Jensen, P.O. Box 297, Hood River, OR 97031. 503/386-3811.

Interstate Plastics, P.O. Box 603, Lebanon, IN 46052. Cabela's, 800/237-4444.

Boats

Here are a few boat manufacturers whose boats I have found outstanding:

Lund, P.O. Box 248, New York Mills, MN 56567, 218/385-2235. Primarily aluminum V-bottoms.

Starcraft, P.O. Box 517, Topeka, IN 46571, 219/593-2500.

Playcraft, Box 870, Richland, MO 65556, 314/765-3265.

Lake Raider, Box 1173, Camdenton, MO 65020, 573/346-4222.

Old Town, 58 Middle St., Old Town, ME 04468, 207/827-5513.

Porta-Bote International, 1074 Independence Ave., Mountain View, CA 94043, 415/961-5334.

Reels, Rods

Cabela's, 800/237-4444. Cabela's sells its own brand of rods which are of superb quality and run considerably less than some of the other premium brands. They have rods of all qualities from cheap to among the best.

Bass Pro Shops, 800/227-7776. "Pro Qualifier."

ABU Garcia, c/o Outdoor Technology, 1 Berkeley Dr., Spirit Lake, IA 51360, 800/237-5539.

Daiwa, 7421 Chapman Ave., Garden Grove, CA 92641, 562/802-9589.

Shakespeare, 3801 Westmore Dr., Columbia, SC 29223, 800/334-9105.

G. Loomis, 1359 Down River Rd., P.O. Box E, Woodland, WA 98674.

Penn, 3028 W. Hunting Park Ave., Philadelphia, PA 19132, 215/229-9415.

Sage, 8500 NE Day Rd., Bainbridge Island, WA 98110, 206/842-6608.

Zebco, Brunswick Corp., P.O. Box 270, Tulsa, OK 76115, 918/831-6938. 33 Classic.

Lures

Jim's Bait & Tackle, Frank Verano, Rt. 44, East Canaan, CT 06024, 860/824-5773.

Hotspot Fishing & Lures, LTD., #3-745 Vanalman, Victoria, BC, Canada V8Z 3B6. Distributed by Scotty USA, P.O. Box 5788, Concord, CA 94524, 510/825-8560.

Tomic Lures, Ltd., Wee Tad, Box 550, Sooke, BC V0S 1N0

Dick Nite, PO Box 2561, Lynnwood, WA 98036. 888/321-LURE. Tremendous kokanee and trout spoons.

Martin Tackle Co., 512 Minor Ave. North, Seattle, WA 98109. Candlefish, small bright orange spoon similar to Mack's Imperial Magic.

Luhr-Jensen, 524 Powell St., Vancouver, BC, Canada, V6A 1G9, 800/535-1711. Also P.O. Box 297, Hood River, OR 97031. Cherry Bobber, Kwikfish (size K7, like Flatfish) Crippled Herring, Needlefish (try the Needlefish), Krocodile, Crystal Krocodile, Kokanee King, Rubber Snubber, Super Duper, Dodgers. Also Les Davis, Dalton, School-O-Minnows, and other trolls. 0000 dodgers.

Vance's Guide & Tackle, Vance Staplin, owner, P.O. Box 4045, Citrus Heights, CA 95611-4045. Vance's Kokanee & Trout Bug. 916/725-2383.

Uncle Larry's Lures, P.O. Box 601923, Sacramento, CA 95860, 916/482-0433. Little spinner strung on mono like a wedding ring lure, but based on colorful glow beads.

Thunderhead Lures, 2984 Lostwood Drive, Sandy, UT 84092, 801/572-0872. Small spoons with a big lip. Very effective.

Whitmann Lures, 3237 E. 45th St., Tucson, AZ 85743. Z-Ray.

Lee Mathews, 1845 Buck Ridge Court, Colfax, CA 95713. 916/637-5041. Firefly, an excellent kokanee bug.

Blue Fox Tackle Co., 645 N. Emerson, Cambridge, MN 55008. Pixee Spoons, Vibrax Spinners (sonic).

Yakima Bait Company, P.O. Box 310, Granger, WA 98932. Rooster Tail, Rooster Tail Lite, Vibric Rooster Tail, Flatfish, Triple Teazer, Freak Spoon (large ones make good dodgers), FST Spoons, Lil' Corky spinner.

Mack's Lure, Box 507, Leavenworth, WA 98828. 509/548-3716. Kokanee Killer, Wedding Ring Spinner, Ring Master, Lucky Cherry, Glo Skunk Fly, Glo hooks (snelled and unsnelled, single and treble), Jeweled Alge, Jim Diamond, Imperial Magic, Double Whammy, Super Wedding Ring Spinner, reflective tape, colored and glow snubbers, Flas Lite Troll.

Bill Arnold, 1165 Garrison St., Lakewood, CO 80215. Arnie's Reflecto Vibrator Lure. This is one of the best kokanee lures around, and it is little known outside Colorado and New Mexico.

Acme Tackle Co., 69 Bucklin St., Providence, RI 02907, 401/331-6437. Phoebe, Kastmaster, Little Cleo.

Panco Lures, 2207 48th Ave., Vernon, BC, Canada V1T 3P9. Cast Magic (like Kastmaster with eye), Diamond Ring Spinner.

Thomas Spinning Lures, Inc., Hawley, PA 18428. "Buoyant" Spoon, #T102-B, 1/4 oz. in fluorescent orange/red/white. Also Cyclone.

Eppinger Mfg. Co., 6340 Schaefer Rd., Dearborn, MI 48126. Dardevle (orange).

Buzz Bomb Lure Corp., 2498 Cousins Ave., Courtenay, B.C., Canada, V9N 7T5, 250/338-5364. Buzz-Bomb, Zzinger.

Fox Creek Lures, 25796 Hwy. 17, Antonito, CO 81120, 719/376-2438. Beetle spin, Stinger spinner, Jiglo jigging spoon, Wraith Spinner.

Bay De Noc Lure Co., P.O. Box 71, Gladstone, MI 49837, 906/428-1133. Swedish Pimple, S.P. Vingla.

Zak Tackle Mfg. Co., 10910 26th Ave. So., Tacoma, WA 98444. #196 NS Doc Shelton DBL lake troll.

Sep's Pro Fishing, Inc., P.O. Box 5356, Vacaville, CA 95696-5356. 707/449-8413, FAX 707/446-3122. Kokanee Kandy, Pro Secret, Pro Dodger, Pro Flashers, Sure Release, Sure Stacker, Pro Trolling Flies, Bite-Me Bug.

Shasta Tackle, P.O. Box 488, Bella Vista, CA 96008, 916/275-2278. Double Dancer, Bug Eyed Stinger, Cripp and Humdinger lures. Shasta is also the exclusive distributor of products from Frisky Plastics.

Frisky Plastics, 1512 So. Oregon St., Yreka, CA 96097, 916/842-1023. Bingo Bug, hook sizes 4, 6, 8, 10. Frisky Fly, hook sizes 4, 6, 8. These small plastic lures are extremely effective.

Attractors

Vance's Guide & Tackle, Vance Staplin, Owner, P.O. Box 4045, Citrus Heights, CA 95611-4045. Cannon ball and large in-line flashers in nickel and gold at very good prices. Superb light dodger. 916/725-2383.

Luhr-Jensen, P.O. Box 297, Hood River, OR 97031, 800/535-1711. 0000 dodgers, plethora of trolls, Jeweled Bead Kokanee Troll #3690, School-O-Minnows #3570. Reflector Tape, including glow.

Real Image, P.O. Box 566, Pacifica, CA 94044, 415/355-8897. Many kinds and colors of reflector tape with holographic images of fish and scale patterns. Real Image also produces spoons with holographic images of fish and scale patterns on them. Some of these spoons, quite large and lifelike, make excellent attractors.

Yakima Bait Company, P.O. Box 310, Granger, WA 98932. Triple Teazer brand dodgers. Excellent.

Mack's Lure, Box 507, Leavenworth, WA 98828. 509/548-5716. Various lake trolls, reflective tape.

Bill Arnold, 1165 Garrison St., Lakewood, CO 80215. Arnie's Reflecto Vibrator Lure. Top-quality trolls in brass, copper, stainless steel with various colors of reflective tape on different blades.

Sep's Pro Fishing, Inc., P.O. Box 5356, Vacaville, CA 95696-5356. 707/449-8413, FAX 707/446-3122. 0000 dodgers in a wide selection of colors. Ultralight lake trolls.

Pop Geer, 439 W. 2nd, Eugene, OR 97401. 4-Blade Indiana Lake Troll.

Silver Horde Fishing Supplies, Inc., P.O. Box 150, Lynnwood, WA 98046. Gold Star Mini Dodger, size 0000, hammered nickel. Many other companies buy their dodgers from Silver Horde. 425/778-2640.

Hildebrandt Corp., P.O. Box 50, Logansport, IN 46947, 219/722-4455. Top-quality spinners and trolls. They use only stainless steel and real gold plating.

Scents

Pro-Cure, P.O. Box 13699, Salem, OR 97309, 503/363-1037. A huge line of very effective scents and means of presenting them.

Berkley Outdoor Technologies Group, 1 Berkley Dr., Spirit Lake, IA 51360. Power Bait, other scents.

Mack's, Box 507, Leavenworth, WA 98828, 509/548-5716. Graybill's Salmon Attractor Scent.

Snubbers

Nat'l Feather-Craft, P.O. Box 19904, St. Louis, MO 63144, 800/659-1707. "Shock cord" looks like mono.

Luhr-Jensen and **Mack's** are good sources of surgical tubing snubbers.

Hooks

Gamakatsu USA, Inc., P.O. Box 1797, Tacoma, WA, 98401. Octopus style (or salmon style) red hooks.

Cabela's sells red hooks by Gamakatsu, Owner, Fenwick, and Eagle Claw. All are quite good. The Eagle Claw hooks work fine for most applications and are much less expensive than the others. E.C. also has red hooks with gold eyes in single and treble. All E.C. red hooks are Lazersharp. 800/237-4444.

Trolling Sinkers

Bead Tackle, 600 Main St., Monroe, CT 06468. (Usually follow with floating lure.) Bead spinners with weight for jigging and shallow trolling. Diamond shaped for casting, jigging, keeled for trolling. Also cylindrical and keeled sinkers without spinner blades.

Luhr-Jensen, P.O. Box 297, Hood River, OR 97031, 800/535-1711. Troll Ease (holds sinkers, acts as keel for lake troll), Luhr-Speed trolling speed indicator.

VENDORS

Cabela's, 800/237-4444. Top-quality products. Fast delivery. Liberal refund policy. Highly oriented to customer satisfaction.

Bass Pro Shops, 800/227-7776. Similar to Cabela's.

Netcraft, 2800 Tremainsville Road, Toledo, OH 43613, 419/472-9826. Lures, tackle, and a good selection of materials for those who make their own tackle.

Offshore Angler, 800/463-3746. Sundry fishing tackle, much of it for saltwater use.

Bait

Vados Express Bait, 15941 Tippecanoe St., NE, Ham Lake, MN 55304, 800/451-2576. Popper Maggots, Eurolarvae, huge mealworms, and other stuff.

Nature's Way, P.O. Box 7268, Hamilton, OH 45013, 800/318-2611, 513/737-2600, FAX 513/737-5421. Spikes (regular maggots.)

St. Joe's Bait, P.O. Box 203, Plummer, ID 83851, 208/686-1234. Spikes.

Miscellaneous Accessories

Idea Development Co., P.O. Box 1290, Issaquah, WA 98027. Tiller handle extension: Allows better trim in a small boat with tiller control; use tiller handle extension and sit in middle seat.

Down-East Sportscraft, Inc., 258 Russell St., Lewiston, ME 04240, (207)783-0421. Excellent quality rod holders, available for various applications and with various types of grips. Handy feature: they open up when you pull up on the rod.

Rainbow Plastic Co., P.O. Box 1861, Ft. Collins, CO 80522. Adjust-A Bubble, for casting and slowly retrieving flies in high elevation lakes like Beaver Creek in Colorado, where kokanee sometimes feed near the surface in the morning and evening.

Bead Tackle, 600 Main St., Monroe, CT 06468. Depth-O-Troll 1000. Unique device aids in estimating lure depth when using lead line, diver, or weight in trolling. Inexpensive and easy to use.

INFORMATION

Kokanee Page on the Internet

Address: http://www.dnc.net/users/nolanr/kokanee.html

From here you can access several more pages on fishing in general and fishing in the Northwest. Some of these are excellent sources of information.

British Columbia Page on the Internet

Address: http://www.nwlink.com/~mmurphy/wbc.html

State Fisheries Agencies

1. Alaska Fish & Game Dept., Capital Office Park, P.O. Box 25526, Juneau, AK 99802-5526, 907/465-4180.
2. California Dept. of Fish & Game, 1416 9th St., Box 944209, Sacramento, CA 95814, 916/653-7664.
3. Colorado Div. of Wildlife, 6060 Broadway, Denver, CO 80216, 303/297-1192.
4. Connecticut Wildlife Bureau, State Office Bldg., 165 Capitol Ave., Hartford, CT 06106, 806/424-3011.
5. Idaho Dept. of Fish & Game, 600 S. Walnut, Box 25, Boise, ID 83707, 208/334-3700.
6. Montana Dept. of Fish, Wildlife & Parks, 1420 E. 6th, Helena, MT 59620, 406/444-2535.
7. Glacier National Park Glacier Park HQ, 406/888-7800.
8. New Mexico Dept. of Game & Fish, Villagra Bldg., P.O. Box 25112, Santa Fe, NM 87504, 505/827-7885.

9. New York Dept. of Environmental Conservation, 50 Wolf Rd., Albany, NY 12233, 518/474-2121.
10. Oregon Dept. of Fish & Wildlife, Box 59, Portland, OR. 97207, 503/872-5268.
11. Utah Div. of Wildlife Resources, 1596 W. North Temple, SLC, UT 84116, 801/538-4700.
12. Washington Dept. of Wildlife, 600 Capitol Way N., Olympia, WA 98501, 360/902-2200.
13. Wyoming Game & Fish Dept., Cheyenne, WY 82006, 307/777-4600.
14. British Columbia, Fisheries Branch, Ministry of Environment, Lands and Parks, 2-780 Blanshard St., Victoria, British Columbia, Canada, V8V 1X4. 250/387-4573.
15. Yukon Renewable Resources, Fisheries Section, Box 2703, Whitehorse, Yukon Y1A 2C6, 867/667-5110.

PRIVATE KOKANEE MANAGEMENT

Project Kokanee, California Inland Fisheries Foundation, 10535 E. Stockton Blvd., Suite H, Elk Grove, CA 95624. (Also Joe "Sep" and Marilyn Henrickson, P.O. Box 5356, Vacaville, CA 95696, 707/449-8413)

BIBLIOGRAPHY

Albert, Ken. *Fishing in Northern California: The Complete Guide.* Fifth Edition. Aptos, CA: Marketscope Books. 1994.

Anderson, Richard. *Trout the Size of Footballs.* Portland, OR: Frank Amato Publications, Inc. 1990.

Beattie, Will; Pat Clancey; Janet Decker-Hess and John Fraley. "Impacts of Water Level Fluctuations on Kokanee Reproduction in Flathead Lake". Annual Progress Report FY 1985. Kalispell, MT: Montana Department of Fish, Wildlife, and Parks. 1985.

Beattie, Will; Pat Clancey and Ray Zubic. "Effect of the Operation of Kerr and Hungry Horse Dams on the Reproductive Success of Kokanee in the Flathead System." Final Report FY 1987. Kalispell, MT: Montana Department of Fish, Wildlife, and Parks. 1988.

Bruhn, Karl. *Best of BC Fishing.* Portland, OR: Frank Amato Publications, Inc. 1992.

Bruhn, Karl (Editor). *BC Fishing Directory & Atlas Freshwater Edition 1995.* Vancouver, BC: OP Publishing, Inc. 1995.

Fothergill, Charles R. and Robert Sterling. *The Montana Fishing Guide.* Woody Creek, CO: Stream Stalker Publishing. 1988.

Wing, Raven and Brooke Snavely. *Fishing Central Oregon.* Bend, OR: Sun Publishing. 1994.

Hubert, Wayne A.; Robert D.Gipson; Timothy C. Modde, and Randall J. Jeric, "Assessment of Spawning Habitat Migration in the Green River and The Potential Influence of Reservoir Drawdown on Kokanee Reproduction in the Flaming Gorge Reservoir System". Wyoming - Utah Completion Report.

Laramie, WY & Logan, UT: Wyoming Cooperative Fish & Wildlife Research Unit (Univ. of Wyoming) and Utah Cooperative Fish & Wildlife Research Unit (Utah State University). 1992.

International Game Fish Association. *1994 World Record Gamefish.* Pompano Beach, FL: International Gamefish Association. 1994.

Jones, Stan (Editor/Publisher). *Washington State Fishing Guide, Seventh Edition.* Seattle, WA: Stan Jones Publishing, Inc. 1995.

Knight, John Alden. Moon Up Moon Down: *John Alden Knight's Story of the Solunar Theory.* Montoursville, PA: Solunar Sales Company. 1992.

Lusch, Ed. *Comprehensive Guide to Western Gamefish.* Portland, OR: Frank Amato Publications, Inc. 1988.

Martinez, Patrick J. and Willian J. Wiltzius. "Kokanee Studies. Federal Aid Project F-79". Fort Collins, CO: Colorado Division of Wildlife. 1991.

Martinez, Patrick J. "Coldwater Reservoir Ecology. Federal Aid Project F-85". Fort Collins, CO: Colorado Division of Wildlife. July 1994.

Martinez, Patrick J. "Coldwater Reservoir Ecology. Federal Aid Project #F-242R-2 (Formerly Project F-85)". Fort Collins, CO: Colorado Division of Wildlife. August 1995.

Outdoor Information Publishers, Inc. and The Post Company. *Montana - Idaho - Wyoming Top 45 Fishing Waters.* Twin Falls & Idaho Falls, ID: Outdoor Information Publishers, Inc. and The Post Company. 1995.

Pennak, Robert W. *Fresh Water Invertebrates of the United States—Protozoa to Mollusca*, Third Edition. New York, NY: John Wiley & Sons, Inc. 1972.

Peterson II, Fred C. *The Outdoor Press, Information for the Pacific Northwest Sportsperson* (Newspaper). Spokane, WA: The Outdoor Press. 1996.

continued on page 166....

BIBLIOGRAPHY *continued...*

Piper, Ti. *Fishing In New Mexico.* Albuquerque, NM: University of New Mexico Press. 1995.

Sample, Michael S. *The Angler's Guide to Montana.* Billings & Helena, MT: Falcon Press Publishing Co., Inc. 1992.

Sheehan, Madelynne Diness and Dan Casali. *Fishing in Oregon Eighth Edition.* Portland, OR: Flying Pencil Publications. 1995.

Steinstra, Tom. *California Fishing—The Complete Guide.* San Francisco, CA: FoghornPress. 1995.

Sublette, James E., Michael D. Hatch and Mary Sublette.*The Fishes of New Mexico.* Albuquerque, NM: University of New Mexico Press. 1990.

Voss, Robert Lee and Gerald Glenn Fuller. *Bob and Jerry's Fishing Guide - Oregon-Over 350 Fishing Lakes & Ponds.* Talent, OR: Bob & Jerry's Regional Graphics Research. 1994.

Washington Department of Fish and Wildlife. "Concise Explanatory Statement Regarding 1996-97 Sport Fishing Rule Proposals. Game Fish and Food Fish." Olympia, WA: Washington Department of Fish & Wildlife. 1996.

VIDEO CASSETTES

Colorado Division of Wildlife. "A Colorado Outdoors Video. Colorado Fishing Hot Spots". Denver, CO: Colorado Division of Wildlife. 1993.

Martin, Roland. "Fishing With Roland Martin: New York Salmon and Florida Red Fish." Hauppauge, NY: Video Cassette Sales, Inc. 1988.

Warburton, Jay S. and Pete Ruboyianes. "How to Troll For Fish." Fort Collins, CO: Warburton Productions, Inc.

White, Charlie. "Why Fish Strike! Why They Don't!" Greenwich, CT: Cabin Fever Entertainment, Inc. 1988.

White, Charlie. "In Search of The Ultimate Lure." Greenwich, CT: Cabin Fever Entertainment, Inc. 1989.